From a photograph of a painting by Lenbach, in Munich
Engraved by T. Johnson

RENÉ FÜLÖP-MILLER

LEO XIII

And Our Times

MIGHT OF THE CHURCH-
POWER IN THE WORLD

Translated by
CONRAD M. R. BONACINA

LONGMANS, GREEN AND CO.
LONDON · NEW YORK · TORONTO
1937

LONGMANS, GREEN AND CO.
114 FIFTH AVENUE, NEW YORK
221 EAST 20TH STREET, CHICAGO
88 TREMONT STREET, BOSTON

LONGMANS, GREEN AND CO. Ltd.
39 PATERNOSTER ROW, LONDON, E C 4
6 OLD COURT HOUSE STREET, CALCUTTA
53 NICOL ROAD, BOMBAY
36A MOUNT ROAD, MADRAS

LONGMANS, GREEN AND CO.
215 VICTORIA STREET, TORONTO

FÜLÖP-MILLER
LEO XIII AND OUR TIMES

This Book was Published in England Under the Title "The Power and Secret of the Papacy"

COPYRIGHT · 1937
BY RENÉ FÜLÖP-MILLER

FIRST EDITION

PRINTED IN THE UNITED STATES OF AMERICA

CONTENTS

CHAPTER ONE

ANATHEMA SIT

I

CANNON thundered on the Aventine and the bells of every Church in Rome pealed out, as eight hundred bishops, patriarchs and abbots moved slowly down the broad and majestic steps of the Vatican. In front walked the choir of the Sistine Chapel, followed by cardinals, abbots and generals of orders, archbishops and bishops, arrayed in shining silver copes and white linen mitres. Next, in their picturesque robes, appeared the patriarchs of the East: the Bulgarian, Armenian, Chaldaic, Coptic and Syrian princes of the Church. Finally came Pope Pius IX, carried down the steps in his canopied *sedia gestatoria*, surrounded by an entourage of the highest ecclesiastical and lay dignitaries. In solemn procession the immense train, representing the whole body of the Catholic Church, moved into the porch of St. Peter's.

At the end of the year 1869 from all corners of the world, wherever the Catholic Faith possessed adherents, bishops came streaming to Rome for the Vatican Council. In hundreds they crossed the snowbound Alpine passes, or voyaged over the high seas despite the winter storms, from England and America, from Africa and from the Far East.

From the early morning of December 8th of that year, the vast nave of St. Peter's had been filled with an immense multitude of people, and now all eyes beheld the dazzling stream of vestments which moved towards the tabernacle above the tomb of the Apostle.

[1]

And when the Pope in his white chasuble ascended the altar, and in a clear, resonant voice audible to all, intoned the *Veni Creator Spiritus*, the whole throng joined in this ancient hymn of Hrabanus Maurus, which implores the Holy Spirit to come down upon the faithful assembled.

The right transept of St. Peter's into which the solemn procession of the Fathers then wheeled had, by the erection of tiers of seats and thrones, been converted into the *Aula conciliaris*, decorated with bright red carpets, silver hangings, gold brocades and pictures. The bishops formed eight rows along the two sides of this council hall, rising one above the other, the Pope ascended the throne erected in the apse, and the cardinals and patriarchs sat down in the large semicircle on either side of him. The raised tribune, however, was reserved for the temporal princes, who by an ancient privilege have the right of being present at the Councils, and of whom the Grand Dukes of Tuscany and Parma had hurried to Rome for this important occasion.

On the altar in the middle of the *Aula* the four Gospels were opened, in keeping with the custom at all great synods from the earliest times. Knights of Malta and Papal Zouaves drew a cordon across the entrance, and, when in the hall of deliberation the first session of the Vatican Council began, the surging of the vast crowd outside was no longer audible save as a distant murmur.

From then on, the bishops of all the kingdoms of Christendom sat in debate, and it took them seven whole months to get through even the first part of the prescribed agenda. The most important points were discussed in fourteen secret general congregations, in the course of which sixty-four speeches were delivered, many of them inordinately long and containing the matter of whole treatises. Twenty-two special discussions were necessary, every sentence wandering backwards and forwards numerous times between commissions of expert theologians, congregations and deputations, until at last, after eighty-six sessions in all, the Fathers were satisfied with all the pronouncements, and in a public session under the presidency of the Pope, gave their *placet* to the "Constitution on the Catholic Faith."

In this "Constitution," the Church solemnly proclaimed her profession of faith in the one, personal God, Who created the world out of nothing, Who guides its destinies, Who manifests Himself in miracles and Who in the books of the Old and New Testaments, has allowed men to share in His revelation, in order that His creatures may learn to know and understand His will and find the way to their supernatural end.

The same profession of faith had once, nearly two thousand years before, filled young Christianity with enthusiastic certainty of salvation — in those days when countless followers of the new doctrine, convinced that the visible world was only a reflection of divine glory, and that happiness in the next life would compensate the Christian for every hardship of his earthly existence, embraced all the torments of martyrdom and allowed themselves to be torn to pieces by lions in the arena, rather than to deny their faith.

This firm conviction that the next world was the true reality set above the transitory phenomena of life received its philosophical and theological formulation in the writings of the Fathers of the Church, and for centuries it passed as the only form of real knowledge. The whole life of the Middle Ages with its political,

[3]

social and economic structure took meaning and form from this belief in the next world. The State was held to be the earthly replica of a *Civitas Dei* established by God; society was organized on the model of the "angelic hierarchy," in successive grades, within which everyone could feel himself in his "natural place" in the service of a divine principle governing the whole universe; and in the consciousness of those times economic problems emerged only as ethical questions.

The Vatican Council of the year 1870, however, passed an Act solemnly confirming its belief in a world order that finds its completion in the supernatural, in that it raised the doctrine of papal infallibility to a dogma. With the proclamation of the decree that a mortal man is endowed by God with the grace of inerrancy, the bishops assembled in St. Peter's affirmed once again the idea of the living connection between the Church and her Divine Founder, between this world and the next, according to the old formula of Tertullian: *"Ecclesia ab apostolis, apostoli a Christo, Christus a Deo."*

The belief that such a grace attached to the papal office had been alive in the Catholic world since the Middle Ages, but it had not hitherto been included among the dogmas of faith. Now, however, the Constitution of the Vatican Council, *Pastor æternus*, declared it "a dogma divinely revealed," that the Pope, "when he speaks *ex cathedra*, that is, when in discharge of the office of Pastor and Doctor of all Christians," is by divine assistance "possessed of that infallibility with which the Divine Redeemer willed that His Church should be endowed for defining doctrine regarding faith or morals."

In this new dogma is embodied the profession of faith in a hierarchy of offices and callings established by

[4]

God, in precisely that irrevocable succession of orders which stretches from earth to heaven, culminating in the *Lumen Gloriæ*, and within which everything and every creature is assigned its *locus naturalis* from eternity.

In this hierarchy of offices the office of the Papacy stands on the boundary between earth and heaven. True, the actual occupant of the papal dignity at any time may be only a weak, erring, sinful man like any other; but his office has been constituted by Christ as the stronghold of the Church, and the Pope who *ex cathedra* (from the Chair of Peter, Prince of the Apostles), speaks to Christendom, stands in the "natural place" of pure truth. Thus, without prejudice to his human weakness, he can never, so long as he occupies this teaching chair, err in the things of faith. He is at this moment only the instrument of a higher power, the medium of a more perfect knowledge that streams down upon him from heaven. Thus it was the intention of the Vatican Council that the dogma of complete freedom from error in any and every decision that issued from the Chair of Peter, should at the same time offer anew to sceptical humanity, torn and distracted by conflicting opinions, a consciousness of the existence of an absolute truth, which would provide it with strength and certainty.

On the day the Fathers assembled in St. Peter's for the final voting on the Constitution *Pastor æternus*, a severe thunder storm descended upon Rome, making the occasion of the declaration of infallibility memorable for the grandeur of its external setting. The correspondent of the London *Times*, who was present at the solemn Act, remarks that this storm must have recalled to many a "superstitious mind" among the multitude present the biblical narratives of the wrathful God of the

[5]

Old Testament. "And so the 'placets' of the Fathers," this description continues, "struggled through the storm, while the thunder pealed above and the lightning flashed in at every window and down through the dome and every smaller cupola, dividing if not absorbing the attention of the crowd. 'Placet,' shouted his Eminence or his Grace, and a loud clap of thunder followed in response, and then the lightning darted about the baldacchino and every part of the church and the conciliar hall, as if announcing the response. So it continued for nearly one hour and a half, during which time the roll was being called, and a more effective scene I never witnessed. Had all the decorators and all the getters-up of ceremonies in Rome been employed, nothing approaching the solemn splendour of that storm could have been prepared, and never will those who saw it and felt it forget the promulgation of the Constitution on the Church.

"The storm was at its height when the result of the voting was taken up to the Pope, and the darkness was so thick that a huge taper was necessarily brought and placed by his side as he read the words: '*Nosque, sacro approbante Concilio illa, ut lecta sunt, definimus et apostolica auctoritate confirmamus.*' And again the lightning flickered around the hall, and the thunder pealed. The 'Te Deum' and the Benediction followed; the entire crowd fell on their knees and the Pope blessed them in those clear, sweet tones distinguishable among a thousand."

2

About the hour of mid-day on the 9th of December, 1869, four hundred and sixty-one gentlemen in black frock-coats, top-hat in hand, solemnly mounted the steps of the Theatre S. Fernando in Naples. On reaching the auditorium they distributed themselves among the seats of the stalls, while on the stage, equipped with a long conference table and chairs, the presiding officials of the meeting took their places.

Amid the applause of the occupants of the hall, Giuseppe Ricciardi arose and, as president, welcomed the assembled company, declaring open the first sitting of the Anti-council of Free-Thinkers convoked by him. That the Roman Church should have dared, Ricciardi continued amid general applause, in this age of enlightenment and progress, again to hold a Council under the pretended guidance of the Holy Ghost, constituted a serious danger to the great cause of civilization and intellectual freedom; it was a question therefore of summoning all enlightened minds to a mighty counter-demonstration, and it was to this end that the present Anti-council had been called. "It lies with us," cried the speaker, "to defend free enquiry against blind faith, unprejudiced reason against religious authority, the independence of the individual against the despotism of the Church. The only means of combating the fresh efforts of the old and irreconcilable enemy of every freedom is a holy alliance of the enlightened of all nations!"

Implacable war against the Papacy, as standing in mortal opposition to all the achievements of mankind, was the substance of the resolution which Ricciardi laid before the Anti-council, and over the wording of which there ensued a lively debate. The resolution formulated by the delegation of free thinkers sent from Paris sounded if possible an even sharper note. Here it was stated that science is the sole basis of all knowledge, and that consequently every dogma founded on any kind of revelation must be rejected.

"Seeing that the idea of a God is the source and

[7]

fulcrum of every despotism and of every wickedness, and seeing that the Catholic Church is the most complete and most formidable personification of this idea and that the total content of her dogmas presents a true denial of human society, the Free-Thinkers of Paris bind themselves to work actively for the speedy and radical overthrow of Catholicism, and to strive for its destruction by all legitimate means, not even excluding revolutionary violence, which is nothing but the justifiable right of defence applied to society."

As with the canons discussed in the *Aula conciliaris* of St. Peter's, the resolutions of the Naples Anti-council were the expression of a mental attitude rooted in bygone centuries and springing from age-old struggles of the human spirit. The hostility to the Church of the free-thinking fraternity assembled at Naples was indeed the result of that great doubt in the truth of dogma which had begun to make itself felt even in the Christian culture of the Middle Ages.

For as the historical distance which separated mankind from the original evangelical experiences of Christianity had increased, the strength of the certainty of faith had proportionately diminished. To an ever-growing number of men the revealed doctrines of Holy Scripture no longer seemed to bear in themselves a wholly sufficient guarantee of their truth. In the feeling of anxiety that arose therefrom there grew an urgent desire for another type of certainty which could be controlled and verified within the domain of the human faculty of cognition. To lead to this, man's inborn reason was held sufficient, and so there now sprung up anew in Christendom that struggle, which had already existed in antiquity, for rational knowledge whose aim was not a certainty derived from faith but an intellectual certainty.

For the satisfaction of this intellectual need there came to the aid of men in the Middle Ages the philosophical and scientific writings of Aristotle, which had been as good as lost for a thousand years. It was then that Christendom made the acquaintance for the first time of a system of thought which from foundation to summit rested on logical reasoning and "proofs." With a comprehensiveness never attained before or since, Aristotle was able to penetrate the whole universe with the intellect and to master all questions and problems; by logical deduction he had created a method which seemed capable of giving the mind certainty in regard to the convictions of being.

The compelling conviction carried by his apparently unbroken and irrefutable deductions, had made the philosophy of Aristotle in other times and cultures — wherever it had been driven in the course of its strange wanderings from the libraries of Syria, by way of Arabian mosques and Jewish synagogues, to the universities of the Christian Middle Ages — the incentive to rational speculation. On all sides it awakened man's latent delight in deductive thought; on all sides it pointed out to minds which no longer found full security in faith alone, a way whereby they could arrive at truth by means of the understanding.

But at the same time, even among the Arabs and Jews, there had arisen that conflict which must inevitably spring up when a culture derived from religious impulses is carried on by rational elements: the conflict between a faith that rests on spiritual experience, on mystical intuition and on authoritative, transmitted revelation, and rational thinking that endeavours to press forward to truth entirely by its own powers.

However, it was in the culture of the Christian West that this conflict kindled by Aristotle produced the most lasting effect and was of greatest importance from the intellectual and historical point of view. When in the year 1085, the army of the Spanish king Alfonso VI entered the Moorish residence of Toledo, the victors found there a circle of Arab-Jewish scholars involved in the most complicated philosophical and theological disputes, all based on points of Aristotelian doctrine. And the same philosophy of reason which had fascinated the pagan mind began at once to cast an irresistible spell over devout Christians, carrying perplexity and unrest even into the contemplative peace of Christian cloisters. One after another the great theologians of the age began to concern themselves with Aristotle and his Arabian interpreters, and one after another all those among them, who deep down in their hearts were no longer quite sure of their faith, succumbed to the dangerous temptation of examining the doctrines of religion with the instruments of doubting reason.

As formerly upon the carpets of Arabian schools of philosophy from Ispahan to Cordova, so now upon the benches of Christian colleges there sat scholars thirsting for instruction, and men of learning argued with one another regarding the value and validity of the rational principle in the domains of faith. With *sic et non* in dialectical battles, in books of sentences and *Summas* it was proved, and again disputed, that the logic and metaphysics of the Greek were in conformity with the dogmas of the Church, or again that they contradicted them.

It was as the "precursor of Christ in natural things, like John the Baptist in divine," that the believers in reason honored their Aristotle. The adherents of the strict doctrine of revelation on the other hand roundly maintained that "the spirit of Christ does not hold sway where the spirit of Aristotle rules." While the Augustinian canons wished altogether to eliminate logical methods from cognition, the Flemish theologian Siger of Brabant defended the views of Averroes, the Arabian commentator of Aristotle, and William of Auvergne and Alexander of Hales sought to rationalize religion by means of the Aristotelian philosophy.

Soon, out of this preoccupation with the logic and natural philosophy of the Stagirite, there grew up that boundless fundamental doubt which strove to put every accepted belief to the test of proof, and which no longer suffered itself to be confined in scholastic formulas. Everything open to the least doubt was now subject to attack, until finally in the seventeenth century René Descartes, the one-time pupil of the Jesuits, declared: "I am at last forced to the frank confession that I must call in question all the opinions I formerly believed. This doubt does not arise from thoughtlessness or frivolity, but from weighty and well-considered reasons."

According to Descartes, doubt is to form the fundamental attitude of reason before every dogma, every phenomenon, every hypothesis; he recognizes its right to examine everything anew without preconceptions, and to reject as uncertain and questionable whatever does not stand this test.

Although the thinkers of the seventeenth century recognized the existence of a second realm of faith alongside that of rational knowledge, the followers of Descartes, the philosophers of the "enlightened" eighteenth century, lay claim to exclusive possession of truth through objective reasoning. With increasing freedom and boldness, the theory was proclaimed that for science there could be nothing supernatural and nothing incomprehensible; that on the contrary every phenomenon, every occurrence, could be explained through natural causes. The existence of a "realm of grace" was flatly denied, and with it the truth and indispensability of divine revelation.

On his death-bed in Holland, the Catholic priest Meslier denied the old faith, and in a confession destined for his congregation, accused himself of having preached lies which he abhorred from his inmost heart. "How I have hated my office as priest, especially the superstitious Mass and the ridiculous administration of the Sacraments, which I have had to discharge with a solemnity that claimed your devotion and your whole faith. What gnawings of conscience has not your easy credulity caused me!"

This priest, under the spell of Enlightenment, was typical of his time. To the whole age the doctrines of religion no longer appeared as revelations of a God Who was Creator and Sovereign Ruler of the world, but as delusions of earlier and as yet insufficiently enlightened generations, or indeed as conscious priestly imposture aiming at the deception and enslavement of men. And, as a result, doubt became intensified into an aggressive hostility towards the whole world of religious ideas and its representative, the Church.

"The unmasking of revelation as the work of men," wrote Voltaire at the time, "and the sawing-through of this human work will bring about the downfall of the Church"; and in a letter to D'Alembert he exhorted the latter to smash the Church, for this "is the greatest service that one can render mankind." Fully convinced of his superior and advanced knowledge, Montesquieu sneered at the "magicians" who "tell the people that three are one and one is three, that bread is not bread, wine not wine." Diderot described the Pope, the "so-called Vicar of Christ," as a "dangerous deceiver," and Holbach declared that on atheism depended the happiness of the world.

For whereas the Reformation and the Renaissance aimed only at bringing about a renewal, a re-birth of old truths and cognitions that had fallen into oblivion, to the Enlightenment "progress" meant not merely a "leaving behind," but also a "destroying" of previous intellectual positions. Old convictions, it was felt, must be eradicated from the consciousness of mankind, in order that nothing might hinder the glorious unfolding of the new philosophy of reason.

Proudly did the French Revolution start the Year One of a new era, regarding all the happenings that precede this date as a succession of dark, unhappy errors.

Doubt, however, did not come to a halt with the proclamation of a "Goddess of Reason." Immanuel Kant entered the lists against the philosophy of the Enlightenment with his "Critique," and extended doubt to the very foundations of thinking, by strictly enquiring into the limits within which reason, according to its own laws, is competent to speak at all. In vain, teaches Kant, does the reason spread out its wings in an effort to "transcend the world of the senses by the mere power of speculation"; for all knowledge must by the very nature of human thinking remain confined to the domain of sensatory perception and the judgments to be derived therefrom.

Thus Kant arrived at the conclusion that all attempts to learn about transcendental things, represent empty and unprovable phantoms of the brain. This view led straight to that "indifferentism," "agnosticism" and "tolerationism" which on principle rejects at the start every consideration of metaphysical problems.

Contempt for every form of religious belief therefore became the basic intellectual attitude of the early nineteenth century. The evolution of mankind was universally regarded as a gradual ascent determined by inevitable laws from lower to ever higher forms of knowledge, and the conviction reigned that the human mind in its inevitable progress could look down on the lower stages of past epochs with pitiful contempt as on youthful aberrations. David Friedrich Strauss saw in religion nothing more than a "weakness of the childhood of humanity," which it outgrows as it advances to maturity, and Schopenhauer wrote that religion would soon depart from European humanity "like a nurse whose fostering care the child has outgrown."

Finally the new age deemed itself in possession of those rational forces which placed it in a position to solve by its own powers all the riddles of the universe; for have not the natural sciences given the human mind means of penetrating into the secrets of the starry revolutions, of chemical processes, of geological and biological evolution? With absolute certainty this generation claimed to have proof that it is not God Who guides the stars, but the sun; that natural laws can never be broken and that miracles are therefore impossible; that the world was not created in seven days out of nothing, but developed out of gaseous vapour in the course of millions of years; that man is not descended from Adam but from the ape, that there exists only matter and no spirit, only this world and no future life; only natural energy and no supernatural force.

And as proof was heaped upon proof to confirm the untenability of the old conception of the world and the correctness of the new, millions in all the countries of Europe took up the fight against the Church in the name of Enlightenment. The new generation championed the law of conservation of energy and the

Copernican system with the same ardour their fathers and forefathers had defended their belief in original sin and in the eternal truth of the revealed Word.

As in the medieval revival of Aristotelian philosophy, rationalism again leaped the bounds of Catholicism and established itself in the midst of the flock of the faithful. In the third decade of the nineteenth century we find the Westphalian parish priest and professor of theology, Georg Hermes, expressly declaring that in his dogmatic studies he had "fulfilled with the utmost scrupulousness his resolve to doubt everywhere as long as possible." This "Hermesianism" spread rapidly among German Catholics and won even the support of high Church dignitaries. Similar teachings were defended by the Viennese Catholic professor of philosophy, Anton Günther, who wished to divest the dogmas of the Church of their absolute character, and submit them to the test of rational examination. In like manner the Munich theologian, Jakob Frohschammer, considered the whole body of Christian doctrine as a matter of natural knowledge and critical speculation.

Some time later Cardinal Count Reisach, Archbishop of Munich, complained that "modern theories" had noticeably lessened the reverence and submissiveness of Catholics towards authoritative dogmas of faith, and exposed them to the danger of "adopting opinions which are in greater or lesser degree opposed to sound doctrine." The new systems of rationalism, naturalism and materialism were now being applied to all subjects of human knowledge, and there was "no longer a science or art, theoretical or practical," which was not "saturated and corrupted" by anti-religious opinions.

"As many Catholic scholars have adopted one or other of these modern philosophical systems, or at least single principles or doctrines thereof, we see today how

[15]

a certain doubt in the choice of means for the defence and development of dogmatic theology is making itself felt in the very bosom of the Catholic Church. And it not seldom happens that in and by their application of the natural sciences and in their treatment of the latter, even Catholic writers and professors, without wishing to do so, corrupt the purity of revealed truth."

*

* *

The scepticism of a new era, which accepted no traditional values on faith, which on the contrary insisted on examining anew everything in this world "without prejudice," could not fail to have a profound effect on the political, social and economic aspects of life in those centuries which succeeded the Middle Ages.

The widespread doubts and questions raised by new social and political conditions had as their result that mankind no longer submitted without demur to accepted regulations regarding rank, that obedience to the authorities of this world as deriving from God ceased to be accepted as an unquestioned duty. As man no longer found his certainties in the metaphysical world, he sought them all the more passionately in those things perceived by the senses and accordingly built his whole existence on the values of this world. Thus both politics and economics gradually broke loose from their moorings to a higher authority and tended to become secularized.

The State was transformed from an institution established by God into a human and practical association formed as the result of a contract between citizens for earthly ends; the Church on the other hand, which as representative of transcendental principles had formerly been placed above all the concerns of life, sank into com-

parative insignificance. Liberalism was the logical results of the conclusions drawn from this sceptical,
"critical" philosophy; as this philosophy teaches that
an agnostic indifferentism is the only appropriate attitude before religious problems, Liberalism proclaimed
the fundamental separation of Church and State. Religiously indifferent, without perception or understanding of the idea of a universal theocracy, the exponents
of the new political order contemptuously relegated the
Church to a place among civil organizations and refused
to grant her any rights above those allowed other sections of opinion or of any influence on legislation.

The severing of the world from supernatural ties was
further effected by the progressive democratisation of
the social structure, and by the replacing of the notion
of rank by the more and more exclusive value set on
the possession of money. Finally the developments of
economic life, of international trade and industrialism
carried this autonomisation of man into the world of
everyday affairs.

Once, in an age when all things were seen in a
religious light, pious theologians did sometimes concern
themselves with economic problems, in order to determine whether — or to what extent — a given industrial enterprise was compatible with the moral laws of
the Church. But now a new science of political
economy was indifferent to such ethical and religious
judgments. Indeed, it professed to believe that the
production and exchange of goods was exclusively the
concern of an individualistic quest for gain, the sole
cause of which was self-interest and the ultimate purpose of which was the material well-being of man.
And it proclaimed the autonomy of the self-reliant industrial person, whose actions were governed wholly
and entirely by a law independent of other laws, and

[17]

whose "economy" formed a system that was self-contained and in no wise dependent upon religion. This spirit of emancipation from all supernatural ties spread even to the domain of moral judgments. It had seemed axiomatic to traditional Christendom that morality derives from religion and subsists because of its dependence upon the divine will. In the modern age, however, this moral theology was gradually displaced by a system of rational ethics detached from religious belief. Bayle put forth the view that moral ideas already exist in the reason and are independent of any idea of God; Kant carried this independence of ethics further, in that he makes the thinking subject the creators of all moral values; while for Comte the moral law coincided altogether with the natural law.

The ethics of the Freemasons in particular are based entirely on human presuppositions and ends: virtue is to be judged solely according to the "natural qualities" of man, and not according to the revealed demands and commandments of God; and the end of moral action is not eternal happiness in the next life, but the perfection of men upon this earth.

3

The conflict between the Church, which seeks to fit everything in the world into an order determined from the Beyond, and laicism, which in its various forms seeks to detach the whole of life from the supernatural, originated ages before when reason for the first time disputed with faith for dominion over the minds of men. It but found scenic expression, as it were, on the two stages of the *Aula conciliaris* and of the theatre where met the Anti-council of Free-Thinkers.

In medieval universities when the great feud started over the teachings of Aristotle, French bishops held a meeting in Paris and described the philosopher of Stagira as a dangerous pagan. Pope Gregory IX stigmatised the attempt to introduce the Aristotelian logic into theology as "absurd and godless," and the papal legate Robert de Coucon flatly forbade the study of Aristotle's *Physics*. Thenceforth, incumbents of Peter's throne neglected no opportunity to inveigh against those philosophers and scientists of the post-mediæval age who sought to proceed along the route of a rationalistic thinking untrammeled by first principles to a new learning dissident from dogmatic teaching.

In the year 1717 the first Masonic Grand Lodge was founded in London, and scarcely twenty years later Pope Clement XII issued his famous Bull, *In eminenti*, which condemned Masonry and forbade adherence to it under pain of excommunication.

The first Pope who mounted the papal throne after the Napoleonic disturbances renewed the fight against the "pernicious errors of our time," and shortly afterwards Gregory XVI directed his attacks against the *pestilentissimus error* of free thought to which mankind had succumbed, against the triumph of "active wickedness, shameless knowledge and dissolute licentiousness."

"Acknowledging Ourselves, to be placed in a situation," continued Gregory, addressing himself to the Catholic bishops, "wherein it may not suffice merely to deplore these innumerable evils, unless We moreover endeavour with all Our might to root them out, We fly to the succour of your faith, and invoke, Venerable Brethren, your solicitude for the welfare of the Catholic flock . . . Our duty it is to lift up Our voice, and to use all endeavours that the wild boar out of the woods do not destroy the vineyard, nor the wolves devour the flock . . . Let us therefore defend in unity of spirit

[19]

this our common cause, or more truly the cause of God."

The election of Pius IX in the year 1846 seemed at first to effect a change in these conditions; for Pius began his pontificate with several attempts to meet the new spirit on various grounds. But he soon recognized how serious was the menace which this era with its "monstrous errors" presented to the Church. Alarmed and angered by the revolution of 1848, which necessitated his temporary flight from Rome, he subsequently raised his voice with increasing violence against the "lying enemies of the Cross," who were endeavouring "with their blasphemies to shake and undermine the foundations of our holy religion, to subvert the religious and social order, and to extinguish every idea of truth and faith."

Pius drew up a whole list of "errors," and in this *Syllabus complectens præcipuos nostræ ætatis errores*, which enumerated and pronounced against eighty propositions drawn from Liberal writings, was summarized and denounced the whole thinking of the new age. Sentence by sentence the papal list of condemnations repudiated all philosophical principles, all theories of political and social life that had been taking form throughout the centuries, and vigorously protested against the mere suggestion that the Pope "can and ought to reconcile and harmonise himself with progress, liberalism and modern civilisation."

*

* *

As often before in her history, the Church again found herself confronted by a spiritual danger which could no longer be overcome by even the most energetic admonitions and fulminations of the Pope alone. In former times, however, when dangerous innovations threatened to unsettle beliefs in the transmitted doctrine, the priesthood of the collective *ekklesia katholike* assembled at a general Council in order to establish as fixed dogmas the decisions of the Church's teaching office and to hurl sentences of excommunication against those who should henceforth refuse their assent to these dogmas.

Thus in the year 325 the Fathers of the East and the West had assembled in the palace of the emperor Constantine at Nicæa, on that occasion when the presbyter Arius had thrown not only theologians but the mass of the faithful into the greatest agitation with his doubts as to whether Christ the Son was of the same substance with God the Father, or only of like substance. For several months, three hundred and eighteen bishops disputed about the "consubstantiality" of the Son and the Father, until finally "Homoousianism" carried the day and became a dogma of the Church.

In later times when Nestorius raised the question of whether the Virgin Mary gave birth to the God Christ or only to the Man Christ, when the Monophysites disputed the doctrine of the two natures of Christ, when the Iconoclasts attacked the veneration of images, when the Beghards questioned man's imperfection and need of grace, when finally the Reformation denied the holy office of the Pope, the doctrine of Purgatory and the possibility of justification by works — on each of these occasions the Church sought defence in a Council. The most recent, the great Council of Trent, lasted for eighteen years and, in opposition to the Protestant movement to cut down the content of faith, dogmatically confirmed Catholic doctrine in all its essential points.

If now, three hundred years after Trent, Pius IX called a general Council, and if this Council met with particularly impressive ceremonies in the Holy City itself, in the church where the Apostle Peter lies entombed, the exceptional solemnity of these arrangements fully corresponded with the occasion. For the danger now confronting the Church surpassed in gravity all previous perils that Catholicism had been called upon to face.

The numerous attacks upon doctrine with which earlier Councils had had to deal, had after all been directed against individual dogmas, but never against religion as such. Now, however, Catholicism was confronted not with a heresy which at any rate assumed belief in God and Revelation, but with a new "enlightened" thinking, a secular philosophy, which was not content with questioning this or that interpretation of a Biblical word, of a passage in the Fathers, of a conciliar decision, but which on the contrary disputed the basic principles of Christianity itself.

At a time when this enlightened, free, undogmatic, relativist thinking was spreading widely and seemed to have the world in its grasp, the Vatican Council proclaimed its firm resolve to hold fast to the Absolute, to revealed dogma and to the belief in a Divine principle governing the whole of existence and uniting all things. In the words of the English Cardinal Manning it was "the widest and boldest affirmation of the supernatural and spiritual order that has hitherto been thrown in the face of the world."

Moreover, in virtue of the higher knowledge vouchsafed to them by the Holy Ghost who descends upon every Council, the assembled Fathers passed sentence of excommunication upon all who denied the dogmas of theology. For the same Church to which her Divine Founder entrusted the "vessel of grace" to be administered, also disposes of a "vessel of wrath" from which she can pour out curses upon heretical doubters and false teachers.

"If any one preach to you a gospel, besides that which you have received, let him be anathema!" With these words of the Apostle Paul begins that long list of excommunications pronounced by the Church upon erroneous teachings, and since the Council of Chalcedon the words *"Anathema sit!"* have been hurled ever anew against doubters. He whom it concerns is held to be divorced from Christ and excluded from the Church.

So now the anathema of the Vatican Council was directed against the principles of modern secular thought, against all those principles upon which rests the philosophical ideas of the nineteenth century.

"If any one shall deny the One true God, Creator and Lord of things visible and invisible; let him be anathema!" begins the list of condemnations drawn up by the Vatican Council, and the Fathers further declare:

"If any one shall say that miracles are impossible, and therefore that all the accounts regarding them, even those contained in Holy Scripture, are to be dismissed as fabulous or mythical; or that miracles can never be known with certainty, and that the divine origin of Christianity cannot be proved by them; let him be anathema."

"If any one shall say that human sciences are to be so freely treated, that these assertions, even if opposed to revealed doctrine, may be held as true, and cannot be condemned by the Church; let him be anathema."

"If any one shall assert that sometimes, according to the progress of science, a sense is to be given to dogmas propounded by the Church different from that which the Church has understood and understands; let him be anathema."

[23]

"If any one shall not receive as sacred and canonical the Books of Holy Scripture, entire with all their parts, as the Holy Synod of Trent has enumerated them, or shall deny that they have been divinely inspired; let him be anathema."

"If any one shall not be ashamed to affirm that, except matter, nothing exists; let him be anathema."

So was repeated eighteen times, like a gloomy refrain, sentence by sentence, that ancient formula: "Si quis dixerit . . . anathema sit."

4

Pius IX's "Syllabus of modern errors," was received with a storm of indignation by all adherents of belief in progress; the document was "a piece of unheard-of impudence," a "counter-manifesto to the declaration of the Rights of Man"; in it the Pope had "thrown down the gauntlet to the whole of modern culture, to the freedom of peoples and of spirits," and finally completed the "divorce" between the Church and the modern world.

Still greater, however, was the excitement over the canons of the Vatican Council in which the collective Church again made solemn profession of her "mediæval" doctrines and, by her dogmatic definition of the infallibility of a mortal man, hurled the most provocative challenge to the critical, unbelieving spirit of the age. In the same year the President of the Vienna Academy of Sciences, the famous physician Karl von Rokitansky, declared in an official speech: "Only after the destruction of the Divine can humanity prosper!"

Not only the frock-coated gentlemen at the Neapolitan Anti-council but all Europe flew into a passion over the proceedings in Rome. In Switzerland demonstrations of protest were organized while in England the great Liberal statesman, Gladstone, voiced his feelings in an article expressing the contempt of the modern world for the spirit of Catholicism.

"Rome," he wrote, "has refurbished and paraded anew every rusty tool she was fondly thought to have abandoned."

And yet the result of the Anti-council of Free-Thinkers must have aroused in the minds of many certain misgivings as to whether the tools of Rome were really so rusty, and those of the Church's enemies so very superior. For at this conference it was again proved that the philosophical view of modern times was, as Schopenhauer had characterised it, a "monster with many heads, each speaking a different language."

What resulted from the Neapolitan Anti-council was by no means the hoped for "Constitution of Free Thought"; on the contrary, within a few hours the debates degenerated into the bandying of empty commonplaces, and finally into a furious wrangle. The first sitting had to be suspended without any agreement having been reached upon the resolutions; while in the succeeding discussions which took place in a hotel, the disputes over the program became so noisy that the proprietor turned the Anti-council out of his rooms, and as all the other hotel keepers of Naples refused to place their accommodations at its disposal, the discussions had to be discontinued.

A sceptical, enlightened philosophy which denied every absolute value was bound of necessity to lack precisely its last inner completeness. Here, where freedom from every *a priori* assumption was the basic principle, where everyone was accustomed to go his own way in penetrating the world's secrets, it was hardly possible to establish forms of organisation of such uniformity and strength as those which the Catholic Church, resting on immutable dogmas, had gradually developed in the course of two thousand years.

Of course since the seventeenth century, there had been no lack of attempts to unite the convictions of the Enlightenment into the basis of a common free-thinking confession, and to organise its adherents into a "rational church." From such endeavours had sprung the brotherhood of Freemasonry. Later, Saint-Simon had dreamed of a Church of the enlightened intellect, in which the spiritual direction of society should fall to men of science, and Comte had even drawn up a program for a "lay anti-church," with a "Positivist calendar," and high priests, dogmas, sacraments, rites and devotions of the positivist reason.

But all these were and remained mere experiments. Whenever the new thought which was achieving such mighty results in the spheres of scientific knowledge and research, strove to evolve an organisation corresponding to and opposed to religious associations, the outcome was at best a pathetic political secret society, usually but a mummery, a stormy session, in any case a confusion of borrowed forms and high-sounding phrases.

So whereas the Anti-council of Naples was compelled after a few days to dissolve without having effected its object or even so much as agreed upon a resolution, the correspondent of *The Times* wrote of the synod which was sitting in Rome at the same time: "Here seven hundred bishops, more or less, representing all Christendom, were seen gathered round one altar, and one throne, partaking of the same divine mystery, and rendering homage, by turns, to the same spiritual authority and power. As they put on their mitres, or took them off, and as they came to the steps of the

[26]

altar, or the foot of their common Spiritual Father, it was impossible not to feel the unity and the power of the Church which they represented."

This unity revealed itself in the days of the Vatican Council in a manner surprising even to Catholics. While the discussions were going on many bishops had frankly expressed their misgivings regarding the proposed dogmatisation of infallibility and had strenuously opposed it. Chief of these was the highly esteemed French bishop Dupanloup, who beheld in the definition of infallibility a grave obstacle to the winning of wavering spirits. "For pity's sake," he had exclaimed in one of his speeches to the Council, "let us not raise barriers and dig trenches between unbelievers and ourselves!"

Cardinal Mathieu took the same view as Dupanloup, and Newman expressed his consternation in an urgent letter from London to Rome wherein he strongly advised against the proclamation of infallibility on the grounds that it was altogether untimely. The English bishop Moriarty expressed a like concern, stating that whereas he had never before felt any anxiety for the Church, he was now made "miserable night and day" by his fear of schism and secret heresy. The Italian, Spanish and South American bishops who pleaded so zealously in favour of the proclamation of infallibility had never, so Bishop Moriarty contended, come into conflict with the unbelieving mind or into contact with the intellectual trends of the time, and consequently could form no idea of the provocative effect such a dogma was bound to have in the modern world.

For the sake of his pet idea, complained Bishop Greith of St. Gall, the Pope was on the point of losing an irreplaceable capital of loyal adherence. Shortly before the decisive last session of the Council, the venerable Archbishop Ketteler of Mayence fell in tears at the feet of the Pope, and implored him to withdraw the fateful dogma: "Good Father, save the Church of God."

Yet hardly had the voting in St. Peter's been concluded, than the American Bishop Fitzgerald, one of the two Fathers who had shouted their *"non placet!"* in open session to the last, rose, advanced to the throne of Pius IX and falling humbly on his knees, said, *"Modo credo, sancte Pater"* — "Now I believe, Holy Father!" And one after another, all the other Fathers followed him, also saying *"Modo credo."*

Dupanloup, who had been the leader in the fight against the dogmatisation of infallibility, now wrote that since the great affair had been decided against them "let all be in praise of the Pope who has been inspired therein as St. Peter and the Vicar of Jesus Christ."

Cardinal Mathieu likewise assented unreservedly with his "whole heart and soul" to the decrees of the Council guided by the Holy Ghost. And all the English, German, Swiss, Austrian, Hungarian and Slav prelates, who had taken alarm at the dogma from the beginning and opposed it to the last from fear of its fateful consequences, now sent their letters of submission to Rome.

However wide might have been the divergences of opinion among the bishops regarding the fitness and opportuneness of the declaration of infallibility, they were nevertheless all united in their belief that the canons of every legitimate Council were ultimately guided by the Holy Ghost, and therefore could not be erroneous or injurious to the welfare of the Church. During the deliberations everyone was at liberty to defend his own particular point of view; separate parties might debate, negotiate, form pacts; but in face of the final decision there could be for them all as believing Catholics only unconditional, convinced acceptance.

The great schism which timid spirits inside the Church had feared, and the enemies of Catholicism had hoped for as a result of the Vatican decree, restricted itself therefore to the defection of the "Old Catholics," who following the example of the Munich theologian Ignaz von Döllinger refused to recognize the Council as legitimate and formed themselves into an independent Church. While in this way some ten thousand adherents were lost to the Pope, many millions of Catholics throughout the world acknowledged as an indisputable article of Faith that the Successor of Peter in his teaching office was endowed with the grace of inerrancy.

*
*   *

"In order to overthrow this Colossus," Voltaire had once said of the Church, "it only needs five or six philosophers to combine and act together." And when the men of the Enlightenment obtained political power over France, they supposed that the Catholic Church, "this old machine," would fall to pieces of itself.

Confident of victory, a member of the Directory of the Republic wrote at that time that the "old idol" would be destroyed, for such was the will of freedom and philosophy. "It is to be wished that the Pope may live two years more in order that philosophy may have time to complete its work, and this Lama of Europe be left without a successor. It is the will of the Directory that when the time comes, the Pope may perish utterly and his religion be buried with him."

As in the meanwhile it had been proved that Voltaire's five or six philosophers did not alone suffice to compass the downfall of the Papacy and its religion, the French Revolution marched on Rome, stuck the Jacobin cap

[29]

on the head of the Archangel Michael, planted the Tree of Liberty on the Capitol, and placed before the Castle of S. Angelo a statue of the Goddess of Reason with its foot upon the papal tiara lying in the dust.

Although the soldiers of enlightened France had ordered the worship of Reason in the Papal States, and prohibited all divine services, although the Roman "patriots" in the Forum, with appeals to the pagan statesmen Cato and Cicero, had proclaimed the dethronement of the Pope and set up a government of Consuls, and finally the Head of the Church, Pope Pius VI had been made prisoner by command of Bonaparte, the spiritual power of Rome still proved unshakable. For the many millions of faithful this powerless, humiliated old man continued to be regarded as the Vicar of God upon earth, as the supreme lord and judge over their consciences, and therefore as the authority which had to determine their attitude before secular powers.

Even Napoleon, who subjugated all power, was gradually forced to recognize that against the Church his weapons were useless. With an invincible obstinacy the oppressed and afflicted Popes of this stormy era refused to bow to the will of the conqueror of all Europe. "I am in your power," said Pius VI on his arrest, "but you have my body alone, not my spirit." And the monk Barnaba Chiaramonti, who was elected Pope in the midst of the worst disorders of war and who took the name of Pius VII, declared no less categorically: "Where it is a matter affecting our conscience, they will obtain nothing from us, though they flay us alive. The Emperor can have us hacked in pieces, but this he will never wring from us." When Napoleon intimated to him that he would be carried a prisoner into France like his predecessor, he received in answer that in that case France "will retain only a poor monk of the name of Barnaba Chiaramonti"; the Church, which lives eternally would then only choose another Pope.

Step by step Napoleon was forced to make concessions to the Church, for he came to realize that without the support of this moral power he would not be able to consolidate his own position. He who began his career as a self-styled revolutionary and Jacobin by declaring that Christianity was irreconcilable with the State, and that the people needed "in place of the catechism a short primer of geometry," was to write a few years later from Milan to his fellow Consul in Paris: "I am going, whatever our atheists may say, in great procession to the Te Deum"; and he admitted that he was always very careful "not to interfere with dogma," that he needed the "ancient Catholic religion, for it alone lives ineradicable in men's innermost hearts," and is able to win people and remove all obstacles. And if he found need of the Church, her supreme Head seemed to Napoleon, the political dictator, a necessity: "If there were no Pope, it would be necessary to invent one."

The man who pursued his mighty plans of domination with such sureness of aim, manifested in his dealings with the Popes a weakness and uncertainty that were usually quite foreign to him; his dominating will was continually crossed and thrown into disorder by a deep respect that ran in his blood. At times with brutal severity, at others with coaxing submissiveness he sought to bend the Pope to his will or to win him to his side. At one time in fury he called him a "raving fool," at another he spoke of him as his "father," his "gentle lamb" and protested how much he loved and revered him. No sooner had he decided to lay claim to the

[31]

imperial dignity than he made a point of having the Pope crown him, yet at the moment of the solemn ceremony he snatched the golden band from the Pontiff's hands and himself placed it on his head.

Leopold von Ranke depicted this strange relationship between Napoleon and Pius VII in words which show impressively the insecure position of the holder of temporal power as compared with him who wields the spiritual authority: "The one in the enjoyment of all the glory and all the power that the earth can offer, full of craft and boldness, sagacity and resolution, allied with all the forces which dominate men; the other, after having been treated for a time with extraordinary deference, soon afterwards deprived of communication with the world, cut off from all, completely isolated. And yet his existence alone was a power. He was allied not with outward and manifest, but with secret inner, forces, which the old habit of faith and reverence over so many centuries throughout the whole of Catholic Christendom, procured him. All eyes followed him; his resistance to violence, his suffering, which aroused general sympathy, had infinitely increased his prestige and surrounded it with the glamour of martyrdom."

To the end, Napoleon was not done with this spiritual power. Even at St. Helena he lamented the fact that his efforts to rule the Pope proved in vain. "If I had succeeded in this, what a lever to world power it would have been! . . . I would have had the spiritual world in my hands as well as the political. . . The control of the spiritual power was the object of all my thoughts and desires. Without it one cannot rule."

After the break up of the Napoleonic empire, Pius VII was hailed as a conqueror. When, on his return to Rome, he reached a part of the fighting line in which the French and Austrians stood facing each other, he drove through the middle of the two camps, and with equal devotion the soldiers of two hostile armies dropped on their knees before him and asked his blessing.

"No other institution," writes Macaulay of the Papacy, which had in such fashion survived the French Revolution and the mightiest autocrat of modern times, "is left standing which carries the mind back to the times when the smoke of sacrifice rose from the Pantheon, and when camelopards and tigers bounded in the Flavian amphitheatre. The proudest royal houses are but of yesterday, when compared with the line of the Supreme Pontiffs. That line we trace back in an unbroken series, from the Pope who crowned Napoleon in the nineteenth century to the Pope who crowned Pepin in the eighth; and far beyond the time of Pepin the august dynasty extends, till it is lost in the twilight of fable. The republic of Venice came next in antiquity. But the republic of Venice was modern when compared with the Papacy; and the republic of Venice is gone, and the Papacy remains. The Papacy remains not in decay, not a mere antique, but full of life and youthful vigour. . . The Catholic Church saw the commencement of all the governments and of all the ecclesiastical establishments that now exist in the world; and we feel no assurance that she is not destined to see the end of them all. She was great and respected before the Saxon had set foot on Britain, before the Frank had passed the Rhine, when Grecian eloquence still flourished in Antioch, when idols were still worshipped in the temple of Mecca. And she may still exist in undiminished vigour when some traveller from New Zealand shall, in the midst of a vast solitude, take

[33]

his stand on a broken arch of London Bridge to sketch
the ruins of St. Paul's."

*
* *

For a time these sentences of the English historian
written in the decades of the Restoration seemed at
variance with historical developments. For in 1848
Liberalism had reached the heights of its triumph
throughout Europe. Again men thought a sentence
of death could be passed upon the Church, as had been
done in the days of the Enlightenment. "The nineteenth century," opined Gustave Flaubert, "will see the
end of all religions. Amen! I shall not weep for any
of them!"

And like the "Reason" of the eighteenth, the Liberalism of the nineteenth century marshalled its armed
forces to bring about the final downfall of Rome, that
citadel of the Papacy, which was considered to exist as
an alien body in the structure of national life and philosophic opinion.

True, before he allowed his troops to march on the
Holy City, King Victor Emmanuel of Italy first addressed a letter in his own handwriting to the Pope in
which he implored him "with the love of a son" volun-
tarily to forego his claim to the Papal States; but as Pius
IX refused as resolutely as his predecessor had done in
the days of Bonaparte, an armed attack was made, and a
few cannon shots directed against the Porta Pia were
sufficient to cause the white flag of capitulation to be
hoisted on the dome of St. Peter's.

Liberal Italy, now anxious to assign to the dethroned
Pope and his Church a place within the general "harmony of interests" which, in accordance with Liberal
ideas, was befitting to an organization with so many

[34]

adherents, promulgated a "Law of Guarantees" which granted the Pope exterritoriality and an annual pension of three million francs. Pius, however, refused to renounce his claim to the temporal power. He showed himself irreconcilable, rejected the Law of Guarantees, put the king and his ministers under the ban of the Church, and as a protest to the world henceforward led the existence of a "prisoner in the Vatican." For Pius IX this voluntary imprisonment lasted for eight years until that day when at an advanced age this Pope, once known for his liberal views but who maintained to the end his obstinate repudiation of the modern world and its forces, closed his eyes in death.

Even in his time Frederick the Great had been of the opinion that were the Papacy deprived of the domains over which it had temporal sovereignty, it must inevitably fall into decay. Thus after the fall of Rome a general conviction prevailed in Liberal circles that the Church could not long survive this change in her hitherto existing form.

Alone of all the statesmen of his time, Bismarck was of a different opinion. In his speeches he repeatedly declared that "for an external sovereign" the head of the Catholic Church continued to exercise an "extraordinarily wide-spread influence" upon nations; that the Papacy was still, as in centuries past, a political power influencing the affairs of this world "with the most determined energy and the most decisive effect."

And if the novelist Flaubert with his passionate belief in progress was convinced of the downfall of all religions, there was another great writer of those times, the Russian Dostoevsky, who, with the insight of genius, perceived that the end of the Papal States was by no means the same thing as the end of the spiritual power of the Papacy. "Oh, for our European politicians and diplomats!" he mockingly exclaimed. "The fallen Pope imprisoned in the Vatican became in his last years such a nonentity that they were ashamed even to mention him, especially the more intellectual and liberal among them. This Pope who received pilgrims and uttered curses even on his death-bed, resembled in their eyes a buffoon who existed but for their amusement." "No," prophesied Dostoevsky, this "greatest idea in the world, an idea sprung from the head of the devil," will certainly not provide its enemies with the joy of seeing it, at the death of Pius IX, "just lie down and die without more ado, passing away in the space of one brief minute."

CHAPTER TWO

HABEMUS PAPAM

I

IN February of 1878, the venerable members of the College of Cardinals, shut off from the outside world, foregathered in the windowless rooms built round the Sistine Chapel, and retired into the mysterious seclusion of a Conclave. And once again the strange spiritual act of birth took place which gave to Pius IX a successor and to the Church a new head.

After only two days' deliberation, the requisite majority of votes was obtained by Joachim Cardinal Pecci, who, having been duly elected Pope, assumed the name of "Leo XIII." At once the canopies over the thrones of the other Cardinals were lowered, and the one over the throne of the Pope-elect alone remained suspended. The golden cross, which each Cardinal wore exposed over his robes for the duration of the *Sedis vacantia*, was quickly hidden in the presence of the new Pontiff, and the secretaries of the Conclave fetched from the sacristy the leather-lined chest containing the garments ready for the Pope-elect. One after the other the Princes of the Church humbly advanced towards the man who until then had been one of their number, but who now stood high above them. Placing on his head the white mitre adorned with diamonds, the "helmet of salvation," they enveloped him in gorgeous robes and put upon his finger the Fisherman's ring with the figure of Peter casting his net. While in the Sistine Chapel, the new Pope, enthroned on the *sedia gestatoria*, received for the first time the kneeling homage of the sacred College, the senior Cardinal-deacon appeared on the outer loggia of St. Peter's and said to the people of Rome assembled beneath: "*Annuntio vocis magnum gaudium: Habemus Papam, eminentissimum et reverendissimum dominum Joachim Pecci qui sibi nomen imposuit Leonis XIII.*"

An infirm old man in his late sixties was Cardinal Pecci on whom the choice of the Conclave fell. As his name resounded with increasing frequency in the reading out of the voting papers, he had been so overcome that tears ran down his deathly pale face, and he had to summon all his strength to avoid losing consciousness.

"I am a feeble old man," he had exclaimed, "I cannot assume so immense a burden! I shall collapse under it in a few days! It is death, not the papal dignity that they propose to bestow upon me!" And after the announcement of his election, the one desire of his friends and supporters was that the frail old man might at least survive the day of his coronation.

However, with Leo XIII there ascended the throne of Peter a Pope who was called upon to guide the destinies of the Church for the space of a quarter of a century. He was to effect in the course of his pontificate a decisive transformation in the relationship of the Vatican to ideas and problems and to the political and social forces of his time, and to provide living proof that the Papacy was as yet by no means prepared "to lie down and die."

*

* *

Righteous indignation had hitherto determined the attitude of the Popes before the developments of modern thought. In tones of stern condemnation Gregory

XVI denounced the *pestilentissimus error* of the new philosophical outlook, in order by wrathful admonishment to prevent "the wild boar from destroying the vineyard of the Lord." Governed by distrust of the new in every form, the Vatican had for a long time banned even such technical achievements as gas-light and railways from the boundaries of its territorial jurisdiction, lest perchance in the train of such novelties the dangerous spirit of progress might creep into the Patrimony of St. Peter.

Thus the Papacy had, as it were, accepted the judgment passed upon it by modern thought, in that it allowed itself to be forced back by the onrush of Enlightenment and Liberalism into the position of a "mediæval survival," of a spiritual power of yesterday, out of touch with life. It seemed as though there could no longer be any understanding between a Church whose dogmas and institutions were affirmed to be fixed and immutable for all time, and a secular cultural system of thought in which everything was conceived to be in constant flux, in a state of ceaseless evolution and development. This enmity had been ratified, as it were, by the declaration of Pius IX that the Pope could not and ought not to reconcile himself with progress.

Indeed the Church and the world now confronted one another in an antagonism of views sharpened to the point of absurdity. If enlightened modern thought with its faith in progress looked back on all the past with contempt and considered the collective cultural achievements of mankind prior to the seventeenth century as useless and meaningless, Catholicism on its side tended in the days of the fanatical *zelanti* to abominate and stigmatise as "error" everything that mankind had achieved since the seventeenth century.

Now, however, there sounded a voice from the Vatican which was raised not to condemn but to reconcile, and the words of the new Pope in regard to the thought and the developments of his epoch possessed an essentially different ring and a different colouring from the enunciations of his predecessors. Long before his elevation Joachim Pecci had spoken, in one of his pastorals as bishop, of Rousseau as the "famous author of the last century," of Galileo as the "man whom experimental philosophy has to thank for its most powerful stimuli," and referred appreciatively to savants like Volta, Linnaeus or Faraday. He had further described the whole science of modern times as the "high stage of nobility and glory to which we now see man to have progressed."

Not only did Pecci feel respect for the theoretical knowledge of his century, but he possessed a sense and understanding of the practical achievements of the modern world. When in his journeys abroad he came into contact for the first time with the world of technical progress, every factory, every railway, even every gas-chandelier had aroused his deepest interest and enthusiasm. "What a miracle!" he had written from Brussels in the forties. "Six iron tracks which pass through Belgium in all directions furnish the kingdom with the most comfortable means of travel imaginable. . . There is nothing grander than these journeys, in which one covers more than twenty miles in the space of an hour; we returned from Namur to Brussels in three hours and a half, during which time we rushed through a distance of some sixty-four miles."

And some decades later, in a pastoral address to the people of his bishopric of Perugia, he depicted the achievements of technical science with truly enthusiastic ardour, and praised them as the fulfilment of the Divine promise in the morning of Creation:

"How noble and majestic does man appear, when he awaits the lightning-flash and causes it to fall harmless at his feet, when he summons the electric spark and sends it as a messenger of his will through the depths of the ocean, over steep mountains, across boundless plains! How glorious does he show himself, when he forces the steam to lend him wings and bear him with the swiftness of the wind over land and sea! How mighty, when by the power of his perceptions he releases this force, and then fetters it again, and brings his control over it to such a point that on prepared paths he is able to give dull matter motion and almost intelligence, so as to put it in the place of man and relieve him of his hardest labours! Tell me, dear Brethren, does not something like a spark of the Creator manifest itself in man, when he summons the light and orders it to illuminate the darkness of the night in the streets of our cities and to adorn the spacious rooms of our palaces with its lustre? But the Church, that most loving of mothers, who beholds all these things, has no thought of putting obstacles in their way; on the contrary, she rejoices at the sight and exults over it."

And among the Latin verses which the Pope liked to compose in his leisure hours, is to be found a poem entitled "Ars photographica," which celebrates in the languages of antiquity the inventive spirit of modern times:

> Expressa solis speculo
>   Nitens imago, quam bene
>   Frontis decus, vim luminum
>   Refers, et oris gratiam.

O mira virtus ingenî
Novumque monstrum! Imaginem
Naturæ Apelles æmulus
Non pulchriorem pingeret.[1]

*

* *

Called to the supreme pastoral office, Leo defined it
as his programme from the beginning to reconcile
Catholicism with modern times, and to make the two
thousand year-old Church work as a living force upon
and within modern society.

It was the express intention of this Pope to join together the united forces of "tradition" and "progress"
which had hitherto been considered as opposed. To
him the new did not necessarily appear as the enemy of
the old, nor the present as the antithesis of the past; on
the contrary, to him true progress was no more than
the historical development of an eternal design which
transcended all human affairs, a development in which
both evolution and permanence took part and were of
equal importance.

And yet even Leo XIII was by no means a revolutionary innovator on the throne of Peter. True, in
disposition, character and in the quality of his mind, he
differed in many respects from the wearers of the tiara
immediately before him, whose endeavours to protect
the Church from the onslaught of modernity had taken

[1] The following translation is taken from *Poems of Leo XIII done into
English verse by the Jesuits of Woodstock College* (Hill & Harvey,
Baltimore, U.S.A. 1886).

ON A PHOTOGRAPH

Sun-wrought image! All may see
Bright and beaming writ in thee
Gracious features, thought-crowned
   brow,
Eyes with living light aglow.

Modern wit is master here:
Not Apelles, Nature's peer,
Could with truer pencil trace
Thy untutored, clear-cut grace.

[42]

the form of a harsh, uncompromising resistance to the new order. But despite the difference in his temperament, his intellectual gifts, his style of expression and attitude of mind, this Pontiff who sought to adapt the Church to inexorable reality, steered the barque of Peter along the same course as his predecessors and pursued the battle for the same end.

In all those questions which have been dogmatically established for Catholicism, he showed himself as unbending and uncompromising as any Pope before him; indeed, in the year 1849, he himself had been a prime instigator of the Syllabus directed against progress, in that at the episcopal synod at Spoleto he had made the motion that the Holy See should promulgate a comprehensive condemnation of the "errors of the age."

Accordingly in his very first papal Encyclical, we find him summoning the servants of the Church "to repudiate categorically all views that are in conflict with the Church's teaching office, however widespread they may be." And with a pointed reference to previous Popes who had never ceased "to reject errors that creep in and to brand them with the apostolic censure," he expressly declared: "We follow in the footsteps of our predecessors and confirm and repeat all those things from this Apostolic See of truth."

Thus although he sought to fit the material culture of the age and its external manifestations in State, society and everyday life into the spiritual structure of Catholicism, this evolution from the instigator of the Syllabus into the Pope of reconciliation by no means signified a departure from the traditional line of Vatican policy. An immovable fixity of principle combined with a due regard for unavoidable changes in men, aims and circumstances can be observed in the Papacy from the

[43]

earliest times. In this permanence in change lies perhaps the most distinctively original secret of this institution and the explanation of the millennial duration of its power.

One Pope has followed another in uninterrupted succession, different men with varying temperaments, each possessing his own peculiar individuality and confronted with new problems peculiar to his time, men not even naturally connected one with another by ties of blood. And yet it would seem as if all these different faces and temperaments show a common feature, as if an eternal undertone rings through their speeches, as though a single great idea determines their decisions and their actions. It is the office that forms their countenances and gestures, that determines their language and activity — that unique office which, planted in earthly spheres, is yet related in all things to an eternal belief in the Beyond.

As earthly stewards of this eternal truth, as custodians of revealed doctrine, the Popes, whether they happened to be fighting with or against their times, have always sought to evaluate the temporal in the light of the eternal. The mission and duty of their office has been determined for them by their belief that above and beyond the sensatory world there stretches over us a higher horizon of divine reality, and that the successor of Peter is called upon to represent this supernatural order within the natural. And this consideration alone has frequently given them their ascendance over the passing developments of the moment.

2

The old and the new, deep-rooted traditionalism and the pressure of the progressive spirit, were forces which mingled variably and inextricably in the experiences of

Leo XIII throughout the whole course of his long career.

Colonel Ludovico Pecci, whose son, the future Pope, was born in the year 1810, dwelled like his forbears in the remote little mountain town of Carpineto, south of Rome, where for generations his family had enjoyed the prestige of a small patriarchal and princely household. Living entirely in the spirit of the past, the colonel still wore a powdered wig and lace-frilled shirts, and as a true subject of his papal lord, he, like his wife, was a devout Catholic untouched by the breath of the "Enlightenment."

Like his parental home, the rest of the environment into which Joachim Pecci was born gave no indication of the mighty convulsions which were taking place at that time in the great world outside. For Carpineto was not only a remote rocky haunt lost in the mountains; it belonged to those States of the Church which like an artificially preserved remnant of the Middle Ages, and in spite of occasional foreign occupations, continued to exist into the nineteenth century.

In this theocracy the Pope was also the temporal sovereign, and priests filled practically all administrative offices. From the Holy Father downwards a hierarchy of officials functioned in cassocks: the diplomats were clerics as were the provincial governors, the judges and the tax-collectors. Thus the whole life of persons who belonged to the *Patrimonium Petri*, was passed, from the cradle to the grave, under the determining influence of the priesthood. No sound from outside penetrated into the twilight stillness of this independent state shut off from the rest of the world.

However, in addition to this spirit of tranquil persistence in the old accustomed ways, the boy was brought into contact from early childhood with an-

[45]

other spirit which was calculated to impress him no less strongly and which soon began to mould his thinking and his character. It was a spirit of sympathetic understanding for many developments of the age and for the realities of the great outside world. A Jesuit school was the place where Joachim Pecci became familiar with a mental outlook that took the new realities into account.

From the date of its foundation in the sixteenth century there had fallen upon the Society of St. Ignatius the mission of bringing Catholicism into line with modern times. It was the members of this Society who, among all the representatives of the Church, laboured most zealously and most successfully to accommodate themselves to changed intellectual and spiritual conditions. As savants they pursued with savants the study of the natural sciences, with a view to deducing therefrom further proofs of the truth of revealed religion; as diplomatists they strove with diplomatists to master the altered methods of the new political science and to place them at the service of the Church in its dealings with temporal powers.

While with tireless energy they defended the teachings and dogmas of Catholicism against both Protestants and the philosophers of the Enlightenment, meeting with remarkable success in their efforts to stem the tide of revolt, it was precisely they who understood most deeply and fully the views of their opponents and realized most acutely when, in the midst of changing developments, they had to deal with the irrevocable. So if in combating hostile teachings the Church did not wholly confine her views to a mediæval conception of world order, but made an effort to maintain a connection with the spiritual evolution of Europe, not the least part of the credit was due to the Jesuits.

During the three centuries of their activity down to the suppression of the Order in 1778, the members of the Society of Jesus, in their numerous schools spread over the whole world, had carried on the education of youth, contributing largely to the formation of the modern Catholic man. The young men who left the colleges of the Society of Jesus bore the mental imprint of their teachers; they were not fanatical enthusiasts and zealots, but flexible, versatile men with a keen sense of reality, whose minds were open to the world, and who for all their piety were well schooled in the arts of diplomacy and in all that makes for an intelligent participation in the world's affairs.

When, after the fall of Napoleon, Pius VII returned to Rome from his captivity in France, he re-established the Society of Jesus with its former rights, and entrusted it with the reorganisation of the school system in the papal territory, which system had fallen into complete decay. The fathers started their teaching activity at Viterbo, and soon afterwards the nine-year-old Joachim Pecci entered this college as a pupil. For the rest of his youth he was to be subjected to the influence of the Jesuit educational system and the Jesuit outlook on world affairs.

*

* *

Later Pecci's career offered him, though only for a few years, an insight into the new life which was developing so rapidly outside the Papal States. Appointed papal nuncio to the court of Brussels at the age of twenty-three, he was suddenly plunged into the midst of one of the centres of the modern liberal-democratic movement, for in the new kingdom of Belgium more clearly than anywhere else in Europe, the era of capitalism on a large scale had begun to assume its definite shape.

[47]

Here, the tremendous developments of modern technical science, which in Rome were considered as distant but dread phantoms, had already transformed the whole existence of men. Already the ore products of the Meuse and Sambre valley were being exploited by a gigantic metallurgical industry; in the huge iron foundries of Ghent and Seraing new smelting furnaces were springing up from month to month; the chimneys of the factories and spinning-mills with their steam engines had altered the entire landscape, and a thick network of railways was crossing the wide Flemish flats and the hilly Walloon country.

Trade and finance had adapted themselves to the new conditions. Hundreds of joint stock companies provided capital for all the newly-established enterprises, ever wider markets were sought for exportation, and at the same time foreign products streamed into the country from England, France and Germany.

But behind this economic organisation with its stimulation of industry and commerce, there was already becoming clearly visible the new social problems: unemployment, hunger, and that distress of the proletarian masses, which undeniably appeared in the wake of economic development in places where liberal ideas prevailed.

Countless families, hitherto able to maintain themselves by the work of their hands, were deprived of their daily bread through the competition of more efficient and cheaper machines. The number of workers whom liberal and capitalist progress expelled from its system swelled daily and they were forced either to accept work at starvation wages or lose their means of livelihood altogether through the increasing mechanization of industry. Crowded together in squalid slums there dwelled masses of hollow-cheeked, starving men and women. In the once flourishing town of Bruges half the inhabitants were completely destitute; more than one-seventh of the Flemish population was in distress; a third of all Brussels had to be supported by public relief.

The young nuncio, fresh from the atmosphere of the Papal States, saw before him not only a fundamentally changed economic world but a new type of State which was equally strange to him.   In the Patrimony of Peter the Pope still ruled with absolute power as an unlimited sovereign from whose decisions and pronouncements there was no appeal.   On the other hand, in Belgium, which had been provided with a liberal constitution, the king was but the crowned head of a people which governed itself in democratic freedom.   Here all destinies and decisions hung on the resolutions of a parliament in which the chosen representatives of the people voted on the continuance of governments, as well as on the passing or rejection of all laws.

In Belgium, in near-by England and the German Rhineland which he visited, as well as in France with which he became familiar as a frequent through-traveller, Pecci soon had to recognise that, with the economic and political and spiritual changes in these countries, Catholicism itself had undergone a species of transformation, and differed very essentially from the rigid conservatism ruling at Rome.

Here the innovations of the age were in no wise accounted hateful, here there was no shutting oneself up against modern ideas and against the world of machines. In constant touch with the Liberal systems of State and society, surrounded by the external forms of modern civilization, the Belgian, like the English and French Catholics, were constantly called upon to defend their convictions and their outlook upon world affairs.   This necessitated their active participation in the democratic institutions of the State, and from representatives of a religious doctrine they were gradually transformed into a parliamentary party.

Moreover, millions of believing Catholics, involved in the economic revolution, had sunk to the state of exploited proletarians, and had joined the ranks of the hunger-stricken unemployed. Accordingly there now arose for the Church, along with Liberalism, a yet more dangerous enemy in Socialism, which preached to the poor a new gospel of violent upheaval and of the coming "kingdom of salvation upon the earth."

On all sides there resounded from the ranks of those men who in the midst of changed conditions were fighting for Catholicism the demand for a "pact" between the Church and the civilisation of the age, to the end that Catholicism might no longer be characterised as the enemy of progressive development, and that further masses of its adherents might not be won over by Liberalism and Socialism. It was already felt clearly in these circles that the opposition between Church and civilisation is not fundamentally necessary, that on the contrary it could be overcome by a correct understanding of the needs of the time.

"Catholic Youth," declared a student of the university of Louvain in an address to the nuncio Pecci, "will provide proof that it is precisely Catholicism which possesses the secret of true spiritual and cultural progress."

Those things which during his sojourn abroad Pecci had considered as interesting and stimulating developments, whose practical applications were matter for thought and consideration, were on his return home to be thrust upon him as subversive forces of the first importance. The year 1848 witnessed that revolutionary upheaval in the Papal States in which the violent onrush of the modern spirit strove to overthrow the last bulwarks that still encircled a survival of the Middle Ages.

Influenced by the February Revolution in Paris, the Roman populace demanded of the Vatican freedom of the press, the building of railways, union with the Italian national State and the appointment of laymen to official posts. Although Pius IX was prepared to yield on several of these points, the result was nevertheless an armed insurrection. The Pope had to flee his capital in disguise and a Constituent Assembly composed of men of liberal ideas proclaimed a Republic.

These events took place while Pecci was at some distance from Rome, in his bishopric of Perugia. Here too the revolution forced its way and there was an uprising of the people. Thus even in his seclusion the future Pope was a witness of that revolutionary attack on traditional authority and religious belief which convulsed the whole of Europe and threatened to destroy all existing institutions.

After ten brief years of calm the spirit of the new age was again thrust upon his attention and this time in a definite form. He was to see the rise of a liberal national State emancipated from the Church; in the year 1860 the United Kingdom of Italy occupied and annexed the northern provinces of the Papal States including the diocese of which Joachim Pecci was in charge.

The Italian authorities with whom the Bishop of Perugia now had to deal were governed by Freemasonic and secular ideals. In conformity with their progressive beliefs, they deemed it an important part of their civilising mission to oust the Church from the official and cultural life of the country, to reduce all her privileges, and above all to wrest from her hands the education of the coming generation.

[51]

Accordingly the royal commissioner, who now took the place of the papal delegate in Perugia, immediately placed ecclesiastical lands and endowments under compulsory State management, closed the monasteries and introduced civil marriage and lay schools. Against all priests who resisted the new order the Italian law proceeded with extreme rigour. Pecci himself was summoned before the courts for having imposed ecclesiastical penalties on certain priests who yielded to the new government on essential points of religious principles.

Thus in the course of his career, Pecci lived through all the diverse phases of that great adjustment of differences between modern times and the conservative forces of the past. The throes of this adjustment were to continue throughout the whole of the nineteenth century, sometimes taking the form of peaceful cultural growth, at others of bloody insurrection, or again of new and powerful political formations.

3

The career of Joachim Pecci is in one respect something of a psychological puzzle. His rise to power does not seem to have followed the lines of natural development as is the case with other great men; his previous career did not lead up, so to speak, to the period when, in a series of encyclicals grandly conceived and broad alike in spirit and scope and in diplomatic transactions conducted with striking skill, he sought to reconcile the conflict between the Church and modern times.

Whereas special gifts and qualities are generally apt to display themselves early in a career, there is scarcely anything in the whole half century that elapsed between Pecci's school-days and his elevation to the purple, which suggests that farsightedness and masterly skill in diplomacy which later contributed to the fame of this

Pope. On the contrary, from the accounts of his friends and relatives, as from his own letters, the picture that chiefly presents itself is that of an energetic, highly cultured cleric who nevertheless judged everything around him or that happened to him, from a somewhat narrow viewpoint.

The paternal home of the Peccis at Carpineto was ruled by the ambition and aristocratic pride of a family whose name was no longer among the most illustrious, and who lived in narrow, indeed almost straitened, circumstances. Thus as he reached manhood the thoughts of the young Joachim were directed first and foremost to fame and success, and the motivation of his actions was a burning desire, stimulated by his relatives, to enhance the lustre of the family name by distinguished achievements and by rapid advancement in the Church.

It does not appear to have been religious fervour but a striving after visible success in his career that first caused him to adopt the priestly calling. "Sound reason and the excellent prospects that offer themselves," he wrote from Rome to his brother, had decided him to become a priest. "I have no doubt that you, with your sound judgment and your eager desire to enhance the glory of the family, will thoroughly approve of my resolve." And on another occasion he assured his brother that he always kept before him as his one main object "to rise in the hierarchical branches of the prelacy, and thus to increase the just respect which our family enjoys in the land."

Every influential connection which his relatives possessed was made to help him in his career, and he even joined a private literary society, as he judged it to be "necessary for the career the first steps of which have been taken." He left nothing untried in his efforts to

[53]

attract to himself the attention of highly placed patrons, for protection was, in his own words, an "indispensable condition" for "rising quickly and surely" in Rome.

Hardly had he received the announcement of his appointment as delegate to the papal civil governor of Benevento, than he proudly wrote home that now the sentries must present arms to him "as to a prince." In everything he undertook and achieved, his gaze remained always fixed on the old palace at Carpineto. He scrupulously sent there every certificate of appointment and every other document that singled him out in any way, so it might be added to the family archives. Immediately after his elevation to the archbishopric, he had painted a life-sized portrait of himself and sent it home with the request that it might hang in the big salon between the portraits of his parents.

As in his efforts at this epoch of his life we fail to find an orientation towards those lofty aims and views which were one day to characterise Pope Leo XIII, so also the beginnings of his political career showed nothing of his subsequent tact and assurance. On the contrary, the actual diplomatic career of Pecci ended after a brief two years in an ignominious failure — with his abrupt recall from the Belgian nunciature and his transfer to the bishopric of Perugia, a change felt by himself and his family to be but a thinly disguised disciplinary measure.

While the young delegate had indeed proved himself a capable administrator who understood how to improve the conditions in the provinces under him, to carry out customs reforms, to start savings-banks and cooperative granaries, to build roads, to organize papal receptions and in such manner to win for himself the good opinion of Gregory XVI, he was by no means equipped for the part of nuncio in Brussels, for he was wholly lacking in any sort of political experience and had not even a command of the French language. Thus scarcely had he arrived in Brussels than he made one mistake after another, although his predecessor Fornari took an interest in him and constantly gave him hints and advice in letters from Paris.

Count Dietrichstein, the Austrian representative at the Belgian court, in an official report to Prince Metternich, made no attempt to conceal the poor opinion held in Brussels of the political talents of the new nuncio: "The Belgian Ministers," he wrote, "greatly deplore the departure of Monsigneur Fornari, who so often saved the situation, in that he knew how to keep the higher clergy within the bounds of prudent moderation. Monsigneur Pecci, on the other hand, makes himself invisible and does not seem inclined to adopt an attitude calculated to exercise a moderating and decisive influence."

Two years later the Austrian Ambassador again discussed Pecci and expressed the opinion that the true interests of religion required that the post of a nuncio in Brussels be filled by a man "of mature character, knowledge of the world, and experience," whereas Pecci, though "the best of good fellows," was young, passive, without initiative, without authority and altogether lacking in that adaptability which was necessary to keep the affairs of his office in order.

At that time the policy of the Belgian Prime Minister Nothomb was mainly directed to the task of holding together as long as possible the two great parties in Parliament — Liberal and Catholic — and to steer legislation along a middle course acceptable to both. Under these conditions, the nuncio was a personage of pivotal importance to the head of the Government, for through him he could give the Catholic party certain unofficial hints and discreetly influence their attitude toward various political questions. But whereas Fornari had lent his support to these tactics of the Prime Minister, the new nuncio lacked the necessary acuteness to grasp aright the hints and suggestions that Nothomb was in the habit of throwing out unobtrusively in conversation. The result was a series of vexatious disputes, and when later the coalition between the Catholic and Liberal parties broke down and the Government was over-thrown through the attitude of the Catholics, Nothomb ascribed the blame for this development—highly dis-pleasing to the Vatican as well—to Pecci's incom-petence. Nothomb's successor was equally dissatisfied with Pecci's diplomacy and ended by urgently request-ing the Vatican to appoint another nuncio.

Moreover, in a question of Catholic philosophy Pecci laid himself open to a painful attack, in that he openly approved of a doctrine taught at the university of Lou-vain at the very time this same tendency was being cen-sured by the Roman authorities.

This succession of blunders and disappointments finally induced the Holy See to recall Pecci from Brus-sels, and when, on his return to Rome, he found Gregory XVI, who had always been well disposed towards him, on his deathbed, he saw an end to all his hopes of continuing in the diplomatic career. Pius IX, whose new Secretary of State, Antonelli, had little sym-pathy with Pecci, showed no sign of fulfilling the hope for a Cardinal's hat which Gregory had held out to him, and he seemed destined to end his life in obscurity as a bishop among hundreds of others.

*

* *

For a whole generation, throughout practically the entire pontificate of Pius IX, Joachim Pecci dwelled in the seclusion of his episcopal palace at Perugia, occupied with the building of churches, with the promotion of pious societies, endowments and brotherhoods, with the guidance and supervision of the priesthood under his charge. Shattered were all his proud hopes of a "nunciature of the first class," of a brilliant career in the world of great courts of the far-flung papal diplomacy, which would mark him out among men and bring distinction to the family name.

Disappointed and embittered, he strove at first to win back the favour of the Curia, set mediators in motion, and paid court to possible patrons. But as time went on he learned to accept his destiny, to take his office as it was, and to devote all his strength to filling it worthily. Gradually there ripened in him the spiritual disposition which found expression in these beautiful words of the sixty-three-year-old bishop, which remind one of Ignatius of Loyola: "Each one of us must be a pliable tool in the hands of the Almighty and be ready to follow at once the voice of the Divine Lamb to whatever place it calls us."

And now in his seclusion and neglect, there came to him quite of itself and almost unperceived that lofty position which had been denied him so long as he strove with such eagerness for fame and success. While he went quietly about the ministration of his office, a halo of greatness, an odor of "election," slowly grew about him, and by degrees his fame spread out beyond the diocese of Perugia until it covered the length and breadth of Italy.

It was only in these long years of retirement that all the experiences and impressions he had collected in his early sojourn abroad seemed to ripen and unfold. The effect of his attaching and powerful personality, felt by the most distrustful sceptics, became stronger and constantly more compelling. He filled the anti-clerical officials of the Italian Government with "an irresistible awe," and from the moment when the state of Piux IX's health took a turn for the worse, rumour with growing insistence designated Joachim Cardinal Pecci as the future Pope.

The wife of the Italian Premier Rattazzi, who passed through Perugia on a journey, wrote—obviously under the immediate impression of her experience—that she had just made Pecci's acquaintance: "I have seen few such expressive heads as his, on which firmness, resolution and strength are so clearly stamped. He inspires alike fear, esteem and sympathy; but fear is the predominant feeling. One would like to love him, but one is afraid to. One thing is certain—he is no ordinary person. His voice is sonorous and full. He has not the princely bearing of Pius IX, but he is equally imposing. His demeanour is majestic and full of dignity; the chief impression one gets is that of asceticism and sternness, but this is softened by a certain benevolence especially when he unbends to children. In a word Cardinal Pecci of Perugia is a grand and impressive figure, and since, as you think, he may one day be our Pope, I shall keep my recollection of him alive in my memory."

When during the last years of his episcopal office Pecci dealt in his pastoral letters with questions of politics and philosophy, the whole world took his words as the utterances of the man who was destined in the near future to ascend the Chair of Peter.

Consequently the Conclave which was to appoint the successor of the deceased Pius lasted but two days. Joachim Pecci became Leo XIII without having had to contend with a serious rival for the highest post in Christendom.

This late rise to greatness, so entirely a development from within, also gradually fashioned the impressiveness of Leo's outward appearance, as we see it in Lenbach's life-like painting — the slight nervous figure with the long slender hands, that infinitely clever head crowned with white locks, the dark piercing eyes, the massive nose, the broad strong-willed mouth. As peculiar and unusual as its rise, was the decline of this life. From the Conclave had issued an old man, who in his weakness and frailty seemed already in the shadow of death. Yet in his advanced age, between his seventieth and ninety-third year, the spirit of this man gained in penetrating keenness as his body wasted away. In this he resembled his antipode who flourished in the early days of the En-lightenment, the great "Anti-pope" Voltaire, to whose portrait as an old man the features of Leo XIII indeed exhibit a certain likeness.

Leo's utterances and decisions also grew continually more impressive in their greatness. And down to the last days of his life this vital activity of his mind never deserted him. After fulfilling the arduous duties of his office from early morning until late evening, he would spend several hours of the night over Dante and Horace, or in giving a final polish to his own Latin verses, as if even the body's last weakness, need of sleep, had left him.

"Ninety-three years old, but upright and unbent, his finely-cut Italian features marble in a pallor that was heightened by his white vestments" — thus does Prince Bernhard von Bülow depict the Pope shortly before his death. "Everything about him had a spiritual aspect. He was very amiable, but in accordance with Italian *gentilezza*, without too much emphasis or officiousness. His poise was perfect, particularly in the sense that no impression from without could shake his equilibrium, let alone endanger it. . . . He had wonderfully fine eyes in which there shone the unassailable faith of the earthly representative of Christ convinced of his sacred mission, and at the same time, something of that impalpable scepticism peculiar to many Italian statesmen of the Holy See, in the council chambers of Venice and Genoa, on the princely thrones of Florence and Ferrara. . . Seldom have I encountered a human being whose spirit seemed so detached as this Pope's; he appeared to have transcended matter and, so to speak, to have reabsorbed it into himself. No taint of earth still clung about him. His robe was no paler than his cheeks, his great eyes glowed with the fire of genius."

And the same deep impression which the statesman Bülow took away from his meeting with the Pope, finds its poetical transfiguration in Stefan Georg's magnificent Hymn to Leo XIII:

Heut da sich schranzen auf den thronen brüsten
Mit wechslermienen und unedlem klirren:
Dreht unser geist begierig nach verehrung
Und schauernd vor der wahren majestät
Zum ernsten väterlichen angesicht
Des dreigekrönten virklichen gesalbten
Der hundertjährig von der ewigen burg
Hinabsieht: schatten schön erfüllten daseins. . .

Wenn angetan mit allen würdezeichen
Getragen mit dem baldachin — ein vorbild
Erhabnen prunks und göttlicher verwaltung —
Er eingehüllt von weihrauch und von lichtern
Dem ganzen erdball seinen segen spendet:
So sinken wir als gläubige zu boden
Verschmolzen mit der tausendköpfigen menge
Die schön wird wenn das wunder sie ergreift.

CHAPTER THREE

SUMMA THEOLOGICA

I

WITH the help of an intellectual system which went back to a thinker for more than six centuries in his grave, Leo XIII sought to reconcile the dogmas of faith with modern thought and to remove that deep antagonism that had grown up between the Church and civilization. The ideas which Thomas Aquinas, the great Doctor of the Schools, set forth in his writings not only determined the philosophy towards temporal affairs which Leo opposed to the rationalistic and materialistic creed of the nineteenth century, but they also formed the unchanging basis for all the pronouncements and acts of a pontificate of vast importance for the modern Church.

In the very year following his election, Leo issued his Encyclical *Æterni Patris*, wherein he recommends to modern times the *doctrina præclara* of Aquinas as the foundation of all true philosophy. With his penetrating yet docile mind, and his tremendous learning in things human and divine, Thomas may be compared to the sun, for "he heated the world with the ardour of his virtues and filled it with the splendour of his teaching. Philosophy has no part which he did not touch finely at once and thoroughly; on the laws of reasoning, on God and incorporeal substances, on man and other sensible things, on human actions and their principles, he reasoned in such a manner that in him there is wanting neither a full array of questions, nor an apt disposal of the various parts, nor the best method of proceeding, nor soundness of principle or strength of argument, nor

clearness and elegance of style, nor a facility for ex-
plaining what is abstruse."

Leo XIII's activities led to what is perhaps a unique
development: in the midst of modern scientific thought
and in an age of full-fledged materialism, a system of
philosophy which had originated in the cell of a mediæval Dominican friar more than five centuries before, began to bear a decisive effect on the historical evolution
of the age. While this "Thomism" had been almost
forgotten outside ecclesiastical circles, and was looked
upon as an obsolete product of the Middle Ages long
ago discarded in the progress of human thought, Leo
acted upon the conviction that there existed in the
past of Catholicism a fundamental element of invariable
truths which in a world that changes from day to day
is unaffected by the flux of time, and which cannot lose
anything of its validity in the passage of centuries. The
conclusions of Thomistic philosophy seemed to him of
this nature and he accordingly felt justified in holding
them up to modern times as guiding principles on the
road to knowledge and world order.

Centuries before these same guiding principles had
restored the *Weltanschauung* of the Christian West
when it was threatened with ruin, for Thomas Aquinas
was born into an epoch when Christendom was being
thrown into vast confusion by the onslaught upon
Faith of rationalistic forces. Mediæval man had long
felt the intellectual need of the acquisition of knowledge
by processes of logical deduction, and in the thirteenth
century the newly-discovered writings of Aristotle provided him with the necessary formulas and methods.
Unfortunately at the same time Christian Europe also
came into contact with all the mass of speculation which
Arabian and Jewish philosophers had fastened to the
Aristotelian theses in an attempt to solve a contradiction

between rational knowledge and revealed teaching which was becoming increasingly apparent.

Thus the notion that a philosophical and a theological truth could exist separately side by side, which was adopted in the seventeenth century by the founders of the new rationalistic and scientific conception of the universe, by Descartes, Galileo and the English deists, had been taught as early as the twelfth century by Averroes. The Arabian commentator of Aristotle maintained that philosophy, which is based on the laws of logical thinking, and theology which rests on Divine revelation, form two absolutely self-contained spheres of experience independent of each other, each of which possesses its own truth and is valid only within its own sphere. Thus with Averroes the same knowledge could be at one and the same time true in philosophy and false in theology.

Moreover, that later phase of the Enlightenment, when reason gained the upper hand over faith and eventually sought to suppress it altogether, was in many ways forecast in the Arabian-Jewish intellectual heritage which fell to the Middle Ages in the time of St. Thomas. As early as the ninth century the Jewish philosopher Saadja ben Joseph, under the influence of Aristotle, had set the authority of reason above the Torah and Talmud and taught that a proposition which was contrary to reason did not become more credible because it emanated from holy writings. To the Bactrian Jew Chiwi, the conclusions of reason seemed so much more certain than the dogmas of faith that he undertook to refute the Bible or at least to interpret it on rationalistic lines. Basing himself on the *Physics* of Aristotle and using almost the same arguments as those developed by modern Biblical criticism, Chiwi disputed the possibility of a world created out of nothing, and taught that the

dealt with nothing!" And Augustine wrote in his *Confessions* that the study of Aristotle had in no wise helped him but rather hindered him, seeing that he had striven in vain with the Aristotelian logic to comprehend God, the "wonderful and unchangeable Unity." "It was falsehood which of Thee I conceived, not truth; fictions of my misery, not the realities of Thy Blessedness!"

When in the ninth century the learned John Scotus Erigena maintained that reason was in a position to refute every doubt in regard to religion, and to prove the truths of religion by logic, he was considered by an assembly of Frankish ecclesiastics as a crazy blasphemer.

But Thomas already belonged to another age, in which rational speculation refused to be excluded from the consideration of the world. True, he did not see in reason the only means to reach the truth, but to him it was no pagan abomination. In contrast to Tertullian and Augustine, he considered the rational intelligence as of equal value with mystical contemplation as a path to the highest truths, and the Church seemed to him strong enough to measure herself with the new intellectual forces which had sprung up in the world, to stand up to them, even to force them into the service of the Faith.

It was to this end that he developed his magnificent system of an "eternal philosophy," which, six hundred years later, Leo XIII adopted anew and made the basis of his own thought and activity.

2

A mighty vision underlies the philosophy of St. Thomas — the vision of an order which regulates the whole universe, from which nothing is excluded, in which there is a place for the Creator and for everything

[66]

created by him. According to a plan laid down by God from the beginning of creation, this order is organized in hierarchical spheres, each one of which ranks above or below the other. Fitted into this all-embracing structure, every motion of life, from the lowest to the highest, has its meaning and end, everything serves in its own way to the perfection of the whole.

Reason also, that mysterious power of man which enables him to advance from deduction to deduction to the last riddle of being, appeared to Aquinas a necessary function in the vast plan of creation and thus it too, if rightly exercised, could contribute to the fulfilment of the Divine Will. For Thomas therefore it showed no diminution of piety, certainly no presumptuous and heretical endeavour to pass outside the closed world of faith, for man to use his reason, that "still small light" which God has kindled in him, for the purpose of striving by eager, tireless contemplation of the systematic connection of all parts of the universe, to arrive at ever more general notions, and finally at the knowledge of the ultimate.

The pagan philosophy of Aristotle, hitherto regarded as the greatest enemy of the Church and the destroyer of devout belief, now became in the hands of St. Thomas a method which, with its logic, with its chain of deductions, with all its intrinsic power to prove and convince, could be used to confirm the dogmas of faith and to defend them against every attack. To be sure, Aristotle himself had declared that by reflecting on the causes of the visible world reason could arrive at the "science of Divine things."

Following the lines of Aristotelian thought, Thomas showed five ways by which thinking can force its way to God by logical deduction, and each of these ways leads to a proof of the fact that this God must exist not only in conformity with the dogmas of faith, but also according to the postulates of reason. From the existence of movement in the world, Thomas, following the example of the philosopher of Stagira, deduced the fact of a Divine "first Mover." Again, from the chain of causes and effects, which cannot each be conceived as extending in an infinite series, there results God as first cause of all caused things; similar conclusions of reason lead from contingency to a necessary Being, from graded perfection in the creature world to Perfect Being, and to the manifest adjustment of means to ends in the processes of nature. In the end logical thought leads to the assumption that there must be a Supreme Intelligence who is author of this teleology.

Such speculations however are intended not merely to show that the existence of God is rationally demonstrable, but that the idea of God is an "inescapable demand" of reason; moreover they may lead to a number of quite definite statements regarding the being and nature of the Creator. For to such a "deducing" mind, God presents Himself as "first Mover" and therefore as *actus purus*, and further as "first Cause" which owes its being to itself alone, as *ens necessarium*, in which essence and existence are absolutely identical, as *ens perfectissimum* and finally as *ens sapientissimum*.

In the eleventh century Anselm of Canterbury, with his *Credo ut intelligam*, had sought to subordinate rational knowledge by faith, but now reason, which had hitherto been regarded as something lying outside the system of faith, became, through its incorporation by Aquinas into the hierarchical order of creation, a *præambulam fidei*. "Faith presupposes reason," teaches Thomas Aquinas. God has given humanity the task of working its way to all truths within its reach, in order that upon these it may construct further knowledge from revelation. Faith is not essentially different from the reason but forms its organic continuation and deepening: "*Actus fidei essentialiter consistit in cognitione et ibi est ejus perfectio.*"

The Thomistic integration of reason in the divine plan is not satisfied however with its inclusion in theology, with its application to proofs of God's existence and speculations upon the last things; it further postulates the fixing of an exact limit to the field of activity marked out for reason. For although Thomas grants the mind capacity to comprehend certain attributes of God, he nevertheless limits this speculative knowledge of God to that part of the divine nature which has manifested itself in the created world perceived by the senses.

Here is the barrier against which all logical deduction must ever beat in vain: A knowledge of what is beyond, of things that lie outside creation, can never be acquired by the path of reason. Mysteries like that of the Trinity, of the Incarnation of God the Son, of original sin, of the Last Judgment or of everlasting bliss, form a "supra-rational" realm before which the natural intelligence retires baffled, and faith has to take its place; for these truths the human intellect cannot grasp, precisely because of their dazzling perfection.

Even here Thomas did not need to part company with Aristotle, in whose *Metaphysics* this statement awaited his discovering gaze: "Our soul's understanding is related to those things which according to their nature are the clearest and most knowable of all even as the eyes of a night bird are related to the bright glare of day."

When the Arabian philosopher Averroes and his Christian followers before Thomas wished to employy human reason without prejudice to faith, they had not been able to bring the cognitions acquired by deductive thinking into harmony with those of revealed dogmatic teaching, and in their dilemma they had fallen back upon the assumption of a "double truth"; Thomas Aquinas, however, sought to prove that reason and revelation represent two forms of expression of the same divine mind, and that consequently complete harmony must at all times rule between them.

God has endowed men with reason in order that they may know Him as their Creator, and God has revealed Himself to them, so that they may learn still more about Him than reason is able to teach them. But since, therefore, both ways, the way of reason and the way of faith, proceed from God and end in God, no real contradiction can ever exist between the one knowledge and the other. Only it may sometimes happen that a wrong use of reason, a false application of our thinking capacity, may cause it to appear as though one truth does not agree with the other.

*

* *

Proceeding from that same conception of a divine order which was the basic concept of the whole Thomistic philosophy, Leo XIII endeavoured, six hundred years later, again to find a place for rational thought in the Catholic scheme of the universe, to enlist science in support of faith, and at the same time to mark off the sphere of its validity as against theology.

In order to dispel the dangers of modern rationalism, it accordingly seemed to him necessary first to remind mankind of what the *magister omnium horarum* once taught regarding the coordination of reason and faith. "Many of those," he wrote in his Encyclical on Scholastic Philosophy, "who, with minds alienated from the faith, hate Catholic institutions, claim reason as their sole mistress and guide. Now, We think that, apart from the supernatural help of God, nothing is better calculated to heal those minds and to bring them into favour with the Catholic faith than the solid doctrine of the Fathers and the scholastics." Thomas in particular by "clearly distinguishing, as is fitting, reason from faith, while happily associating the one with the other, both preserved the rights and had regard for the dignity of each; so much so, indeed, that reason, borne on the wings of Thomas to its human height, can scarcely rise higher, while faith could scarcely expect more or stronger aids from reason than those which she has already obtained through Thomas."

Wholly in the spirit of Aquinas, therefore, Leo also extolled reason as a divine gift in so far as it keeps within the limits of its own proper sphere, and he too considered reason and faith in no wise as opposed to each other but as complementary means of knowledge working together in harmony. As regards all those matters which "the human intelligence may perceive, it is equally just that philosophy should make use of its own methods; so far is the superadded light of faith from extinguishing or lessening the power of the intelligence that it completes it rather, and by adding to its strength renders it capable of greater things."

Such an integration of the physical sciences into the totality of the possibilities of knowledge provided for in the divine plan can, in Leo's opinion, only serve to advance in pre-eminent degree the spiritual progress of mankind. "For the investigation of facts and the contemplation of nature is not alone sufficient for the profitable exercise and advance" of the physical sciences. "But when facts have been established it is necessary to

[71]

rise and apply ourselves to the study of the nature of corporeal things, to inquire into the laws which govern them and the principles whence their order and varied unity and mutual attraction in diversity arise."

But for Leo as for Thomas, such cognitions are beyond the reach of the unaided reason; at this boundary it is always necessary for reason to be completed by the truths of faith. The sooner the world returns to this conviction, the more quickly will the chaos of opinions which has resulted from "unprejudiced thinking" give place once more to a sure and settled Christian order built on solid foundations.

3

The ideas behind freedom and equality, liberalism and democracy, those political shibboleths of the nineteenth century, were the direct result of the rationalism of the Enlightenment, and the Church had hitherto shown towards all the suspicion she was wont to cast on every manifestation of enlightened rationalism. Leo however considered these doctrines in the light of the Thomist conception of the divine order, and arrived at the conclusion that liberty and democratic government stand in conflict with religion only when, and in so far as, they are not properly integrated in the great collective whole.

If the drift of public and domestic affairs, as it presents itself to the eye of the modern Catholic, points on all sides to a "lamentable and fatal" deviation from the Church, the blame for this development can only be ascribed, in the words of Leo's Encyclical, to the erroneous theories respecting our duty to God and our responsibilities as men, which "originating in the schools of philosophy, have crept into all the orders of the State and have been accepted by the consent of the masses."

For since it is in the very nature of man to follow the guide of reason in his actions, any error which the mind may make, is apt, Leo contends, to be quickly followed by a corresponding error in practical action. Thus "looseness of intellectual opinion influences human actions and perverts them."

Because human reason has succeeded through the findings of the natural sciences in penetrating divers secrets of external creation and in making them serve the requirements of life, "there are some who, in their overestimate of the human faculties, maintain that as soon as man's intellect becomes subject to divine authority it falls from its native dignity, and, hampered by the yoke of this species of slavery, is much retarded and hindered in its progress towards the supreme truth and excellence." Accordingly they repudiate "the most sublime truths," reject the "divine gift of faith" and seek to banish the authority and sovereignty of God from society.

To oppose these disorders, Leo resolved to employ the Thomist method of classification to bring about an understanding between the Church and the social ideals and demands of the new age. For in the principles of Thomism, "freedom," that great shibboleth which had inspired the century of liberal rationalism and was now proving so effective in all the new social institutions, is of value provided it is not removed from its place in the great connection of things and singled out as the supreme ideal.

Nothing lies further from the mind of the Church, declared Leo in his Encyclical *Libertas*, issued in the year 1888, than not to give their proper due to the demands of the age and the new requirements of society, or to stand in the way of modern forms and improvements, many of which, on the contrary, she gladly

[73]

welcomes. In their good elements modern claims to liberty have always been sanctioned by the Church, and this applies especially to the natural freedom to act as one pleases in choosing the best means for the end proposed.

This freedom however must always be considered in its higher connection with the good of the whole, and, precisely on that account, it must be submitted to the guidance of eternal principles, without which it is impossible for man to know when he is using his freedom for a good end or an evil one. Accordingly freedom demands, as its necessary correlation, law, which alone makes its right application possible. Freedom, coupled with the law governing the whole world order, which in its highest form manifests itself as God's moral command, but in its earthly form as political regulation, should help man to arrange his life in harmony with the necessities of human and political association and ultimately with the will of the Creator, and so contribute to the perfection of the universe.

But without the limitation of such a law set above the pleasure of the individual, no freedom is conceivable, seeing that man stands in an eternal relation to the whole of creation around him, below and above him and to his Creator.

"To refuse any bond of union," says Leo, "between man and civil society, on the one hand, and God, the Creator and consequently the supreme Law-giver, on the other, is plainly repugnant to the nature, not only of man, but of all created things; for of necessity all effects must in some proper way be connected with their cause."

This ordination towards God as his last goal contributes essentially to the dignity of man; for indeed to be man means to stand at the frontier of the finite world, to behold this frontier and to know that beyond it lies another reality, and that only from that reality beyond does everything on this side derive its meaning, end and fulfilment.

*
* *

When the enlightened man of the nineteenth century with his ardent belief in progress wished to show how completely he had emancipated himself from all supernatural ties, and to give visible proof of his autonomy and security, he could proudly point to the marvellous progress of material civilization which constituted the great triumph of natural reason. Precisely on this account, the Church, prior to the days of Leo, had considered this material progress as the expression of a hostile principle, and preceding Popes had rejected it with profound mistrust and had done their utmost to prevent its entry into the Patrimony of Peter.

Leo, however, hoped, through the medium of Thomist philosophy, to bring this aspect of modern existence into positive relationship with Catholic religious life. In the days when St. Thomas Aquinas created his philosophy, there had also existed what appeared to be an essential contradiction between the religious and the material world, and like the Church of the early nineteenth century, the pious theologians of the thirteenth had considered the revolutionary changes begun at that time in the material world as a falling away from true religion. Yet Thomas had understood how to resolve the discord and re-establish harmony.

As the period known as the Middle Ages approached its wane a pre-capitalistic economic life had begun to develop whose activity grew less and less compatible with that renunciation of the world taught by the exponents of patristic doctrine. The merchant class of the flourishing towns became wealthy; Crusaders, bankers and Jews spread the nets of commerce over the whole known world; on all sides commercial houses and shipping companies came into being; and despite ecclesiastical prohibition, usury, which had hitherto been proscribed as a grievous sin, became more and more general.

Confronting this increased commercial activity stood a Christendom which, under the influence of the Platonian philosophy transmitted through Augustine, regarded all earthly things as meaningless phantoms. According to these ideas earthly existence should be ordered solely according to the divine destination of the soul, towards the "heavenly Zion" and in the pattern of the Redeemer. Thus an ascetic and renunciatory attitude towards the things of life prevailed. So severe was this attitude that a profound conflict between Church and world was bound to arise.

With Thomas, however, the "entelechy" doctrine of Aristotle won the victory in Catholicism over the "idealism" of Plato, and the relationship of the Christian to surrounding reality was thus transformed. For whereas Plato transferred all realities to an eternally unattainable world of "archetypes," Aristotle had taught that everything bears within it the perfect idea of itself as "entelechy," as innate disposition, formal principle and end, and that everything in this world is governed by the endeavour to perfect itself towards this final end, which is its perfect realization.

With the adoption of this philosophical outlook, the earthly order, which in the eyes of the Middle Ages before Thomas had passed for a world of illusion, appeared as an orderly phenomenon of profound teleological significance. Creation spread itself out before the vision of Aquinas with a new nobility, a new sanctity, for each element constituted an unbroken gradation of forms on an ascending scale of perfection, each form being endowed with the predisposition towards the next in rank above it.

Accordingly the creation which is tangible and perceptible to the human senses presents itself as a world of equal sanctity with that which is erected in harmonious correspondence with it in supernatural spheres. Just as human reason arrives at God in an unbroken chain of syllogisms, so too is there a "hierarchy of ends" ascending step by step from formless *materia prima* to the divine *actus purus* freed from all material dross.

This view of the "hierarchy of ends" leads however to the recognition of an independent sphere of earthly things; for here too, as in the cognitive faculty of the intellect, Thomas distinguishes two grades, one ranking above the other. Every created thing not only goes back to the divine *causa prima*, and not only serves an ultimate other-world end, but it is also produced, within the chain of earthly connections, by a definite secondary cause perceptible to the reason, and there belongs to it a proximate practical end of existence. Thus below the great creative causes and transcendental ends which ever remain a Divine mystery, there is revealed an order of secondary causes and proximate ends, in which man can act according to his reason, according to his judgment and according to his designs.

Although the last end must always remain the beatific vision of the *veritas prima*, or the first divine Truth, nevertheless earthly activity is by no means contemptible and futile as the Augustinian-Platonist ascetics had supposed. On the contrary, if pursued in the right spirit, it becomes a rational movement of the creature towards God. For the same God who has bestowed upon man the light of reason in order that with the help thereof he may know God as the Creator, has also endowed him with the gift of rightly comprehending his earthly mission. Here, however, it is by no means essential always to have in view with every action the absolute idea of the highest good; it is sufficient to do on each occasion what is right in reference to the immediate actual task before one, for with that alone man already adopts the position proper to him in the great hierarchy of ends and fulfils the mission that God has allotted to him.

Certainly in that higher grade of ends which is elevated above the realm of secondary causalities and finalities, human purposiveness falls short. We cannot attain to the "realm of grace," where the great first and principal cause is alone at work, through our willing and doing directed to temporal ends, but solely through the miraculous power of the Sacraments. But there is no gulf separating these two spheres of divine first cause and the earthly secondary cause from each other: the realm of grace continues the realm of earthly conditioned causes and ends as a harmonious progression; it crowns and perfects it: *"Gratia non destruit naturam sed supponit et perficit eam."*

In the *Summa theologica*, that great work of Aquinas, everything that offers itself to the *magister omnium horarum*, from the most trifling problems of everyday life up to God Himself, be it in the practical order or the sacramental, in the sphere of knowledge or of faith, is considered a part of the great plan of creation. For "the entire content of the Christian religion" was to form the subject of this work, so that God may be truly known "not merely as He is in Himself, but also as being the principle and end of all creatures and particularly of rational creatures."

In thirty-eight treatises with six hundred and thirty-one questions, about three thousand articles and ten thousand objections, Thomas handles his vast programme, point by point, according to the strict scholastic method. Each individual question is first formulated in a *titulus articuli*; next under *videtur quod non* are detailed all the objections that speak against the author's view; then with a *sed contra* begins the refutation of these objections, and out of this is finally developed the demonstration proving the particular solution which Thomas himself holds to be the right one.

In this way the *Summa* in its first main section thoroughly examines the theological and philosophical questions relating to the existence and attributes of God, after which it proceeds in the second part to investigate the problems of ethics as of human activity within the *causæ secundæ*. And there Thomas, to a far greater extent than any of his Christian predecessors, takes into consideration the chain of circumstances by which every action is determined, the manifold intentions by which it is guided, so that many parts of the *Summa* actually form the basic ideas for a modern political order.

But this keen and penetrating observation of practical life as conditioned by time is always subordinated to the great final end, the knowledge of God and the ordination of man to God. Thus the system of St. Thomas removes the tension between the claims of religion and the pressing demands of everyday life, inasmuch as here the earthly and the heavenly, worldly wisdom and Divine wisdom, practical life and asceticism, are no longer regarded as irreconcilable opposites, but as two allied stages of an all-embracing coherence.

*

* *

It was in this spirit that Leo accepted material civilization with its whole mass of worldly entanglements for mankind as Thomas had done six centuries earlier.

Whereas Pius had repudiated the suggestion that it was necessary for the Pope "to reconcile himself with progress," Leo willingly recognized the "immense progress" that has been made in modern times "towards securing the well-being of the body and of material things." All that the arts and sciences have done to advance the culture of our age, every improvement that "ministers to the refinements and comforts of life," everything that promotes honest trade and the increase of public and private prosperity, every true liberty which is "worthy of the sons of God and nobly maintains the dignity of man"—all these things, Leo solemnly asserts, have the Church's full and unequivocal blessing.

Accordingly the achievements of progress and civilization ought to be neither neglected nor despised. Rather is it our duty to watch over these things with care, to promote them and hold them in high esteem, for they form a "precious store of blessings," inasmuch as "they entirely represent means which are good in themselves and have been willed and destined by God Himself for the great profit of mankind."

This temporal world can, however, only attain its dignity and holiness, if it too is fitted into its proper place in the hierarchy of ends and ultimately ordained to the Divine last end of all existence. For through a civilization conceived purely as an end in itself mankind has never yet been able to satisfy its "thirst for perfection. Man has made matter subject to himself, but matter has not been able to give him what it does not possess."

The idea that what was required was to fit a culture that had become autonomous and a purely worldly affair into supernatural relations, and that in order to do this it was necessary always to "turn one's eyes to the intention of the Creator," constantly recurs in the pronouncements of Leo XIII from his first Encyclical *Inscrutabili Dei consilio* down to the Apostolic Letter *Pervenuti* of the ninety-two-year-old Pontiff. Repeatedly the Pope expressed his conviction that without this binding of natural creation to the supernatural world, no civilization is capable of bearing "worthy fruits."

In his instructions to Cardinal Rampolla on the appointment of the latter as Secretary of State in 1887, the Pope wrote that the enemies of Catholicism appealed to civilization and progress as if they provided an argument for the destruction of the Church. "Fundamentally, however, only that can represent real progress for man, which leads to his spiritual and moral perfection or at any rate does not oppose it."

Thus all the utterances of this Pope which express his philosophy have in common a basic idea — that it must again become possible, as it was in the thirteenth century, to resolve all apparent contradictions between reason and faith, between the striving after temporal ends and the higher ordination to a divine end, by a loftier view co-ordinating both, and thereby to re-establish that harmony between the two which had been achieved in the *Summa theologica*.

"While, therefore," writes Leo at the conclusion of his Encyclical *Æterni Patris*, "We hold that every word of wisdom, every useful thing by whomsoever discovered or planned ought to be received with a willing and grateful mind, We exhort you, Venerable Brethren, in all earnestness to restore the golden wisdom of St Thomas, and to spread it far and wide for the defence and beauty of the Catholic faith, for the good of society and for the advantage of all the sciences — *ut Sancti Thomæ sapientiam restituatis et quam laterrime propagetis*."

CHAPTER FOUR

SAPIENTIÆ CHRISTIANÆ

I

WHEN in the last years of his life Pius IX, as "prisoner of the Vatican," gave audience to cardinals, prelates and pilgrims, the corpulent old man whose countenance was disfigured by erysipelas, whose swollen legs covered with running sores had long since made walking impossible, never missed an opportunity of fulminating from his bath-chair against the pernicious and devilish errors of modern times. Neither age nor illness could change his conviction that it was his sacred duty to fight, protest and curse to the last. "They say I am tired," he once declared; "yes, I am tired of all the many injustices I see, but I have no intention on that account of laying down my arms or shirking the fulfilment of my duties!"

And yet before his death it had dawned even upon this irreconcilable anathematizer that the Church would soon have to meet the unalterable realities of the world with other means of action. For when one of the dignitaries of his entourage once asked him what counsels he proposed to leave behind for the next Pope, he replied: "Everything around me has changed: my system and my policy have had their day, but I am too old to revise my orientation. That will be the work of my successor."

And this successor did, in fact, immediately after his coronation, undertake "to revise his orientation" and to lead the Vatican along the lines of a policy based on the conciliatory ideas of Thomism. But what with Thomas had remained theory, philosophical hypotheses, a mass of questions, sentences and deductions, and which in the course of six centuries had been further read and commented upon by countless generations of zealous Christian scholars, this Pope now turned into a programme for practical and political action.

The first and most urgent task which presented itself to the new supreme head of the Church was the settling of hostilities between the Holy See and temporal powers, in which Leo found the Curia involved. For in the decade prior to his elevation "the age-old struggle for power between kingship and priesthood" which in Bismarck's words, "had filled the whole of European history since the Middle Ages," had burst forth anew with the greatest violence.

From the times of St. Augustine the Church had kept before her eyes the picture of a *Civitas Dei*, in comparison with which the secular State, as it actually existed, could never be anything but an imperfect copy of that divine society. To assimilate as far as possible the world to this *Civitas Dei* seemed to be the mission of the Church established by Christ, which therefore considered herself authorized to claim supremacy over all earthly rulers in the name of her Divine Founder. Thus the "two-sword-theory" of the early Middle Ages taught that God had entrusted to the Church the two swords of the spiritual and the temporal power, and that the Church had of her own free will passed on one sword to the princes of this world. The temporal power stood therefore in a permanent relation of vassalage and subordination to the spiritual power embodied in the Papacy.

But kings and emperors had soon repudiated such a limitation of their power, and on their side laid claim to supremacy over the ecclesiastical authority in their own sphere of power. Thus from the beginning of the tenth century the tension between the two powers had been growing increasingly acute, and this struggle for supremacy, which first came to an open breach in the great "Investiture Dispute" of the eleventh century, took the form of a series of dramatic conflicts which are brought down to us in the pages of history.

We may read how the mighty Pope Gregory VII arose and declared in his *Dictatus Papæ* that the Vicar of Christ was entitled to "extend his foot to be kissed by all princes," to depose disloyal emperors and to release subjects from their allegiance to the lords of the land. When Henry IV refused to submit, Gregory excommunicated him and, invoking the Apostle Peter, solemnly pronounced formal interdict against the German king: "I in thy stead, bind him with the bond of anathema; thus acting in confidence on thee, that the nations may know and acknowledge that thou art Peter, that upon thy rock the Son of the living God hath built His Church and the gates of hell shall not prevail against it."

A year later King Henry, deserted by all the great ones of his realm, appeared at Canossa in the hair-shirt of a penitent, to implore from the Pope the removal of the ban and with it the restoration of his kingdom. Soon after the picture changed again; Rome was conquered by Henry's armies, the Pope imprisoned in the Castle of S. Angelo.

In the days of Frederick Barbarossa this reversal of triumphs and humiliations had been repeated; at one time the Pope had to flee before the fury of the Emperor, leaving St. Peter's a blazing ruin, at another the temporal ruler fell at the feet of the spiritual; the Emperor held the Pope's stirrup.

In the firmament of heaven — so, in the year 1200, declared Innocent III, the great opponent of King Philip Augustus of France—God set the greater light to rule the day, and the lesser one to rule the night, and just as the sun with its own bright, warming and animating light ranks above the moon, so has the head of the Church the prerogative over the head of the State, who can only borrow his light from the former. And again at the beginning of the fourteenth century the full claim of the Holy See to supremacy over the rulers of this world was renewed in the Bull *Unam sanctam*, wherein Boniface VIII again claimed for himself the right to appoint and depose temporal sovereigns; yes, it was necessary to salvation to believe that "every human creature is subject to the Pope."

At the zenith of the papal power such rights were not only proclaimed, but were also exercised in practice. When King John of England sought to oppress the Church, the Pope solemnly deposed him from his throne, and the French king was instructed from Rome to carry out this sentence upon the Englishman by force of arms. Only when John on his knees swore homage to the papal legate and declared his kingdom to be a tributary fief of the Papacy, did the Vicar of Christ remove his interdict. The same Innocent III who thus forced the British monarch into subjection, exacted payments of tribute from the rulers of Aragon and Portugal, gave the Bulgarians and Wallachs a king and settled political conflicts in Poland, Hungary and Norway. Even in the days of the great discoveries and voyages, it was the Roman See which fixed the line of demarcation between the colonial spheres of influence of Spain and Portugal, thereby acting as judge over the partition of the earth.

*
* *

Dating from the establishment of absolute forms of government, and particularly later in the era of liberal and nationalist currents of thought when European humanity tended more and more to emancipate its existence from all supernatural ties, the States resisted those papal claims to supremacy with growing obstinacy and ever increasing success. The expulsion of the Jesuits from practically every European country at the end of the eighteenth century sealed the triumph of the sovereign will of the individual State over the old idea of theocratic universal monarchy; for it was precisely as the professed champions of the latter that the members of the "Society of Jesus," those "shock troops of the Pope," had incurred the distrust and displeasure of rulers and statesmen of enlightened absolutism.

When therefore Bismarck was able to complete his great work with the coronation of the Emperor at Versailles, the Chancellor considered it necessary to make clear at once that this new empire did not represent a continuation of the old "Roman Empire of the German nation" which went back to the installation of Charlemagne by the Pope, and in which the old conception of the Christian universal monarchy had always survived. "In two directions," runs an official statement issued by Bismarck, "the new German Empire must categorically renounce all the traditions of the old: it has nothing to do with hierarchical or theocratic, nothing with cosmopolitan tendencies. It is a secular, a national State."

In the Vatican, however, the memory of the great days of papal power remained alive. The Popes still deemed themselves the supreme lords and judges of everything that went on in the whole of Christendom, and demanded from monarchs and ministers just the same submission to their decisions as from the clergy and body of the faithful. Accordingly Piux IX wrote

[86]

to the Emperor William, the Protestant ruler of the newly established "secular and national" German Empire, that the Emperor too, like every baptized Christian, belonged irrespective of his confession and position "in some sort of way to the Pope."

Such claims on States which had long felt themselves emancipated from all ecclesiastical tutelage, resulted inevitably in the demand of the nineteenth century that the "age-old struggle for supremacy" be fought to an issue. Especially was this true in the new German Empire which had just torn itself away from union with the Catholic monarchy of the Hapsburgs, and whose millions of Catholic subjects had hitherto been accustomed to take from Rome not only their philosophical outlook but their political instructions as well.

The canons of the Vatican Council, raising the Pope to a position of absolute authority within the Church and subordinating the collective episcopate of the world to the Sovereign Pontiff, had been widely regarded in the non-Catholic circles of Germany as a danger to the national integrity and sovereignty of the Empire. Bismarck declared in a decree of the year 1872 that the Pope, as a result of the Vatican Council, had "in principle taken the place of every individual bishop," and that it rested solely with him also to usurp the same powers in relation to governments. "The bishops are now only his instruments, his officials without personal responsibility; they have become in relation to governments the officials of a foreign sovereign and of a sovereign too, who in virtue of his infallibility, is completely absolute — more so than any absolute monarch in the world."

In face of the influence of this foreign sovereign, however, Bismarck emphasized his conviction that "in the kingdom of this world" the State has "rule and precedence." In order to secure this rule and this precedence in Germany, Bismarck initiated in the seventies those "May Laws" (so-called from the date of the first group issued on May 15, 1873), which were intended to place a number of important branches of Church administration under the control of the Government. For in the opinion of the Chancellor, it was only by securing permanent control of the Catholic Church, of her hierarchy, pastoral office and educational activity that the State could feel assured that the loyalty of the Catholic population and their obedience to the Government, would not be endangered by "ultramontane influences."

Piux IX, however, with his prepossession in favour of traditional ideas concerning the universal power of the Church, was not the Pope to endure in silence such political interference with ecclesiastical organization. He angrily refused his consent to the German laws, and forthwith summoned the faithful to resist with the utmost determination measures which seemed to him unjust and tyrannical. And so in a short while there broke out on German soil that grave conflict between the State and the Catholic Church which, under the name given it by Virchow, has become famous in history as the Kulturkampf.

At that time German Catholics were deluged with a constant stream of governmental and ecclesiastical regulations which were diametrically opposed to one another, the one forbidding what the other ordained. If Falk, the Prussian Minister of Education, ordered the bishops to notify the provincial governors of every new appointment of a parish priest, then the Pope strictly prohibited the fulfilment of this obligation. If the government insisted that all candidates for the priesthood should pass an examination at a State university, then the bishops refused to allow candidates even to enter for such examinations. If the government introduced a special supervision over Catholic schools, then the clergy made a point of ignoring any and every regulation made by the inspectors appointed for the purpose.

With each year the conflict grew more bitter, both parties resorting to harsher and more violent measures as the struggle continued. The courts imposed fines on the bishops who refused to obey orders, and these in turn remained unpaid by order of Rome; the bishops had their goods seized, and when there was nothing more to seize, they went to prison. Refractory priests had their stipends suspended by the government; in return the Church forbade the clergy to take part in the celebrations of Sedan Day. In the Reichstag the Catholic party organization of the Centre, always viewed by Bismarck with profound distrust, grew under the leadership of the ardent Catholic parliamentary orator Ludwig Windthorst, into the bitterest opponent of the Chancellor.

The result of the Kulturkampf was to make impossible any agreement between Church and State with regard to the filling of vacant sees and livings, since the government rejected on principle all the candidates of the Vatican, while Rome on her side refused to nominate personages acceptable to the government. Thus the Catholic dioceses and parishes were gradually deprived of their pastors, and owing to the lack of priests recognized by the civil authorities, marriages in many places became impossible. This in turn caused the government to introduce obligatory civil marriage by new legislation.

This struggle for power gave rise to the strangest scenes: archbishops disappeared for years behind prison walls, an over-zealous police confiscated the consecrated Host from the altar, secret services were held by loyal

Catholics at dead of night, as in the days of persecution in the early Church. In after years Bismarck himself wrote with bitter irony about the grotesque picture afforded by "honest but clumsy gendarmes with spurs and trailing sabres chasing nimble and light-footed priests through back-doors and bedrooms."

However while the Kulturkampf was in progress the Chancellor still held the view that it was impossible to arrive at an agreement with the Church "without effacing to a certain extent the secular power and in a manner which the German Empire at any rate cannot accept." And in the Reichstag he proudly exclaimed: "Do not fear, we will not go to Canossa either in body or in spirit!"

Meanwhile Pius IX sat in the Vatican and angrily characterized events in Germany by the most vivid language suggested by the Church's trials in other ages. Thus he spoke of a "Diocletian persecution," and called Bismarck a "second Nero," a "new Attila," "a scourge of God." And he reminded a body of German pilgrims of a threatening saying of the Old Testament, in that he intimated that no one could tell "whether the little stone might not soon be loosed from on high which should break the feet of the Colossus."

*
* *

"Myrmidons of the apostolic chamber," "abettors of the Papal Chair"— with such expressions of suspicion and distrust did Gladstone, Bismarck's great English contemporary, characterize the Catholic priesthood in the days of Pius IX. In his opinion too, they seemed to be striving everywhere to bring the State under subjection to an absolutist foreign power. Never, he contended, had the Roman clergy ceased to uphold the extravagant claims of the mediæval Papacy to temporal sovereignty, or to plot and intrigue in the interests of "papal aggression."

For England herself, who had shaken off her dependence on Rome in the reign of Henry VIII, the influence of the Catholic Church had of course ceased to be a danger ever since the last armed attack of Catholicism had suffered defeat with the Armada of Philip of Spain. But there was still a point in the British Empire where the power of Rome made itself permanently felt, and this point was Ireland.

"My body to Ireland, my heart to Rome, my soul to heaven!" with this testament upon his lips Daniel O'Connell, Ireland's great "Liberator," had passed away in the year 1847 ; and after him the feeling of their country's close ties with the Papacy remained alive in the hearts of the Catholic Irish. Even in the last decades of the nineteenth century, the difference in religion between the Irish people and their English conquerors formed one of the strongest motives for unrest in the land, and the Irish clergy lent the weight of their influence with the masses to the nationalist movement directed against English rule.

Gladstone who had made reconciliation with Ireland a main plank of his political programme, beheld in this "Ultramontanism" of the Irish a serious obstacle to his plans, for time and again he saw his efforts at settlement break down because of the obstinate resistance of the Irish Catholics engineered by the Vatican. Filled with resentment, he wrote that in view of the mingled policy of violence and cunning that emanated from Rome he found it impossible to conform to the mild language of diplomatic usage. He spoke in terms of the utmost harshness of Piux IX and he recalled the fact that once before, in the sixteenth century, Rome had endeavoured, albeit in vain, to stir up the Catholic subjects of the British crown to treasonable support of the country's enemies.

And as in Germany and England, so even in such a good Catholic State as Austria, the leading politicians came to feel the influence of the Church upon the people to be a dangerous limitation of the ruler's sovereignty. Thus a third of the great conservative Powers of Europe saw itself forced to take up a hostile attitude towards Rome in order to cope effectively with "Ultramontanism" and Vatican claims to supremacy. Scarcely had the Vatican Council declared the Pope infallible and possessed of autocratic powers over the whole Church, when the Austrian Government replied by denouncing the Concordat with the Vatican and passing a series of important laws against the independence of the ecclesiastical administration, which laws Pius IX condemned "as essentially and wholly hostile to the Church."

*

* *

With Leo XIII a fundamental change took place in the attitude of the Vatican towards the powers of the State. Leo had learned from Thomas Aquinas that there exists in the world a sphere of secondary causes within which man is free to act according to the dictates of his reason. In this sphere Thomas had included the State in so far as it has to look after the public order and the physical welfare of its citizens. In all departments of secular life the temporal power appeared to Aquinas as completely sovereign and in no way subordinated to the supremacy of the Church.

In conformity with this conception Leo then sought to draw a line of demarcation between the faculties of the State and those of the Church. As custodian of the

Faith, the Church should certainly be entitled to regard herself as above the State in all questions affecting religion, but it did not befit her to lay claim to a similar supremacy in matters of secular legislation. By his acceptance of a viewpoint which assigns to the State an autonomous sphere of activity withdrawn from every measure of ecclesiastical influence, Leo finally broke with the "two-sword-theory" of the Middle Ages, and showed himself ready to "render to Cæsar the things that are Cæsar's."

The practical results of this change of attitude soon made themselves noticeable. In a short time the apparently unbridgeable conflict between the Vatican and the German Empire reached an amicable settlement. Concessions and counter-concessions followed each other in rapid sequence. The Church withdrew from all those fields which in the light of Thomistic distinctions belong to the State's autonomous sphere of authority. The German statesmen on their side found themselves ready to withdraw their encroachments upon the domain of purely ecclesiastical administration and, taking with one hand and giving with the other, to repeal the "May Laws."

In the fourth year of Leo's pontificate, Emperor William I announced to the Prussian Landtag the resumption of official diplomatic intercourse and the cementing of friendly relations with the Vatican, and soon afterwards Leo was able to inform the College of Cardinals with great joy that peace with Prussia had been restored. "The Pope is a wise and moderate man," Bismarck now said, and he seized the first opportunity that offered to proclaim to the whole world the high esteem in which he held Leo XIII.

In a diplomatic conflict that broke out between Spain and the Reich over the occupation of the Caroline islands by Germany, the Chancellor formally requested the Pope to act as arbitrator. Such a request had not been made to the Vatican since the beginning of modern times. Leo, therefore, expressed his appreciation of the honour paid him and cordially agreed to assume the office of judge; and in making his award, he was careful to see that the interests of Germany in the disputed islands received every justice. And on the German Chancellor, whom only recently Pius had called the "new Attila," Leo conferred the decoration of the Supreme Order of Christ ornamented with diamonds and created him a Knight of that Order.

"A series of successes has crowned the Pope's activity in relation to the European Powers," wrote A. P. Iswolski, at that time Russian special envoy at the Vatican, to his Foreign Minister, "especially as regards Germany which has resumed diplomatic relations with the Holy See, moderated its anti-Catholic legislation and given the Pope the satisfaction of letting him play the rôle of arbitrator in a question of international importance."

But even in the internal politics of Germany, where prior to Leo every interference of the Vatican had been looked upon as an intolerable encroachment, a significant transformation now took place. Bismarck himself showed no hesitation in appealing to the Pope for his support when he was anxious to carry his new Army Bill in the Reichstag. Whereas only ten years before, Pius had summoned the German Catholics to resist the executive power, Leo now urged the Centre, who were opposed to the Bill, to vote in favour of the government.

The altered situation found its most typical expression amid the pomp and splendour of a royal banquet. At the court dinner with which, on March 22, 1887, the ninetieth birthday of the Emperor William was celebrated at his Schloss in Berlin, Monsignor Galimberti, the official representative of Leo XIII at the jubilee celebrations, was among the number of those invited. Just as the guests were taking their places at table, the Empress Augusta turned to Galimberti and said to him: "Note this occasion well, Monsignor, as it has a historical significance; for today is the first time that an envoy of the Pope has come to sit at the table of the king of Prussia." And behind this peaceful picture of the prelate dining with the Emperor, the scenes, now tragic, now ridiculous, of that "Diocletian persecution" to which the Catholic Church in Germany had for so long been subjected, completely disappear.

With the pontificate of Leo XIII a similar change took place in the relations of the Vatican with Austria and even with England. When the Irish nationalists started fresh agitation and began organizing an anti-English boycott, the new Pope at once ranged himself categorically on the side of the government at Whitehall, and sharply reminded the Irish Catholics that the legitimate authority of the State must be recognized and respected unconditionally. In no case, therefore, he wrote to the Archbishop of Dublin, was it permissible for the people to disturb public order by acts of violence, and it was the duty of the clergy to restrain the faithful from all such revolutionary action.

In the English Parliament this move of the Pope's met with immediate acknowledgment. In much the same language as Bismarck's, Gladstone began to extol Leo's good intentions and truly paternal spirit; and when on the occasion of Queen Victoria's jubilee, the Vatican sent the nuncio Ruffo-Scilla to London, the reception accorded him at court and in government circles was no less friendly than that accorded to Galimberti at the same time in Berlin.

[95]

It was possible for the Pope to settle the conflict between Church and State on the basis of a just division of authority only in cases where the temporal power simply demanded its independence and where basically the matter resolved itself into a dispute regarding the frontiers of the political sphere of authority. There were two countries, however, in which, during those last decades of the nineteenth century, it was more than a question of where the Church's sphere of power left off and that of the State began.

In France as in Italy the purely secular philosophy of "enlightened" rationalism had seized possession of political power and was now seeking to displace religion by an "anti-Church" directed solely to earthly ends. Here therefore Catholicism was confronted by a spirit which claimed for itself the sum total of existence and which was able to use all the means of power provided by governmental authority for the enforcement of this claim. What Saint-Simon and Comte had dreamt of — the subjection of mankind to a "church of intellectuals," the replacement of "metaphysical unrest" by positivism, the setting up of an "ideocracy"—these things French and Italian statesmen now sought to realize by means of political laws and regulations.

To these men the doctrines of religion appeared as the relics of an infantile stage in the development of human thought, as superstition and priestly deception, and their opposition thereto seemed a fight for progress, for the emancipation and higher spiritual development of mankind. From the spirit of this new world of "positivist" thinking was to be abolished for all time everything that pointed beyond the kingdom of the "human" to a supernatural world.

In their pride, these free-thinkers boasted that "after centuries of ignorance" the time had come to kindle the "torch of reason." Followers of the Enlightenment, of Voltaire and Comte, these politicians firmly believed in the infallibility of reason, in unlimited progress, in almighty science.

The Society of Freemasons gave this philosophy its forms, organization and its international solidarity. And as Freemasonry contributed very substantially to the formation both of United Italy and of the Third French Republic, Freemasons frequently occupied the chief political offices of these Powers.

Italy in particular had mainly the Lodges to thank for her national deliverance and unification, beginning with the "march of the thousand," which had been instigated by the Mason Mazzini, prepared by the Masons Crispi, Bertani and Lafarina, and led by the Mason Garibaldi, and for which the Mason Fauché had provided the ships. "Freemasonry will lead humanity forward," Garibaldi was wont to assert. "The constant application of its sacred principles must lead to the brotherhood of all nations."

Among those who had participated from the beginning in all the dramatic actions, daring stratagems, assaults, campaigns and marches of the masonic and nationalistic struggle for independence, was the man who now, when victory was won, rose to the post of Prime Minister of the Italian kingdom — Francesco Crispi. To him — the creator and far-sighted promoter of Italy's position as a Great Power — the Catholic Church was "il nemico eterno," the eternal enemy to be fought to the death. That the power of the Papacy still prevailed in the world was, in Crispi's view, a circumstance that did not speak well for human intelligence; but Freemasonry must and would succeed in making all

Italy close its ranks so as to form a "phalanx against the medievalism of the Church."

A Freemason like the Italian Crispi was the Frenchman Léon Gambetta, whose personality, oratory and forceful activity for ten years determined the course of the newly-established French Republic. As Crispi spoke of the "nemico eterno," Gambetta coined for his hatred of the Church the phrase, "Le cléricalisme, voilà l'ennemi!" The struggle against Catholic influence on the destiny of new France formed a substantial part of Gambetta's public activities. He travelled from town to town trying to stir up the enthusiasm of the French people for a programme of reform which provided for the complete separation of Church and State.

The tireless agitator with the massive head framed in a shaggy growth of hair and beard, who hammered unceasingly into the heads of the masses the idea that the struggle for the freedom and civilization of France and of the world demanded the complete overthrow of the Church, became, in the years of his rise to the premiership, a symbol of the anti-Roman attitude of the enlightened, positivist masonic Third Republic. "He wants to be the master of those who no longer have a master," says Alexandre Dumas of him; "he thinks himself the God of those who have no God."

*

* *

In the days of the Kulturkampf the Prussian government introduced compulsory civil marriage; yet both the Emperor and his Chancellor felt this step to be undesirable in itself and only justified as a measure of necessity imposed by the circumstances of the struggle. At the time, Alexandrina, the Emperor William's sister, wrote to her imperial brother entreating him not to permit civil marriage to enter Germany. "Please hold fast to the word of the Lord," she pleaded, "do not allow yourself to be led astray by the spirit of the age, which produces such ideas. No blessing will follow such a course. At The Hague I was present at one of these civil marriages. It is revolting, for it is purely human, and there is nothing divine in it." And in his reply the Emperor told his anxious sister that he himself took the same view of this "unhappy civil marriage" as she did: to him too it seemed "the first step in the abolition of the holy and Christian"; but unfortunately "the intolerance of the Catholic priesthood" made it a necessity of State.

For governments, however, which aimed at the setting up of a lay anti-Church, civil marriage formed an important point of the programme for exactly the same reasons that made this institution seem so dubious to the German Emperor and his sister. For them it was precisely a question of "abolishing the holy and Christian," and of making of marriage "something human, but not divine." With the help of the registrar of marriages, a sacrament sanctified by God was to be transformed into an act of legal administration, to become the averment of a purely earthly, legal and personal relationship.

It was in the field of the education of youth, however, that the Church and the lay State came into the sharpest conflict, for here the question was: under whose spiritual direction was the rising generation to be placed? If the educational question was of exceptional importance even to conservative Powers where it was only a matter of fixing the frontiers between religion and State, in countries where the Enlightenment aimed at the final destruction of the Church it became the focus of the whole great conflict. Indeed the disciples of progress always hoped for the final "victory over all errors" by the rising generation as a result of its proper upbringing.

Accordingly by means of laws and coercive measures of every kind, the compulsory lay school was established both in France and Italy. In the French elementary schools religious instruction was replaced by ethical courses of a purely secular character; the use of crucifixes and other religious symbols was forbidden, and from the new schoolbooks the word "God" was as far as possible omitted.

Owing to sharp differences on the educational question, matters had already come in the days of Pius to an open rupture between the Vatican and the liberal Government of Belgium. The Belgian bishops solemnly condemned the school regulations introduced by the State and refused absolution to all teachers in State schools. In return the Belgian Government handed the nuncio his passports and recalled its chargé d'affaires from the Vatican.

Laicism employed every possible means to destroy the position of the Church, and finally the French Government proceeded to the forcible expropriation of the monasteries. When the silent white Carthusian monks of the Grande Chartreuse refused to surrender their ancient house to the authorities, the red-breeched soldiers of the Republic were ordered to march into the remote valley and drive the obstinate monks from their monastery.

While in France the military was being mobilized against a religious community withdrawn from the world, the hatred of the anti-clerical and Masonic elements for the Church was being demonstrated with equal violence in Italy. Adriano Lemmi, the Grand Master of the Italian Lodge, openly declared that the Law of Guarantees, which assured the Pope exterritoriality, must be abolished, in order that "the stones of the Vatican may be scattered," and no memory of the Papacy be left. With Crispi's approval and under the auspices of the Freemasons, a monument was erected in Rome in 1888 to Giordano Bruno, the Renaissance philosopher and opponent of the Church, and the spot chosen was the Campo de Fiori, opposite the former papal Cancellaria where Giordano Bruno had been burnt at the stake by order of the Inquisition. The address at the unveiling of the memorial, which took place in the presence of Crispi, was delivered by Jakol Moleschott, the German champion of extreme materialism, and the ceremony was made the occasion for the most violent denunciations of the Papacy.

Thus Leo XIII too was forced to regard Masonic laicism as the Church's most dangerous enemy, and to attack this implacable opponent with no less vigour than his predecessor. For him especially, precisely because he lived wholly in the world of Thomistic ideas, any compromise with Freemasonry was impossible. Deeply imbued with a conception of the universe in which all temporal ends appear in relation to a supernatural destiny, Leo saw in that "ideal of humanity" which limits all objectives to the world of the senses and takes no account of a metaphysical order, an illusion and a falsification of truth. Accordingly he attacked in the strongest terms the efforts of the Freemasons "to pass off a part for the whole," and to remould the life of man on an earthly ideal that seemed to him basically false.

Hence in the Encyclical *Humanum genus* launched by Leo against Freemasonry, we find a sharpness and violence of tone that is quite unusual in this Pope. The whole system is referred to as a "vast evil" aiming at the destruction of religion and morality alike, and Freemasons are accused of having as their "ultimate purpose, the utter overthrow of that whole religious and political order of the world which the Christian teaching has produced." Seeking to build up a new order on naturalistic principles, they wish to "do away with the expectancy of the joys of heaven and bring down all happiness to the level of mortality, and, as it were, sink it in the earth."

With a "rashness unknown to the very pagans," they have in public matters no care for religion, and in the arrangement and administration of civil affairs show no more regard for God than if He did not exist. "They are boldly rising up against God Himself and are planning the destruction of Holy Church publicly and openly."

"With the greatest unanimity," complains Leo, "the sect of the Freemasons also endeavours to take to itself the education of youth. They think that they can easily mould to their opinions that soft and pliant age, and lead it whither they will. . . Therefore in the education and instruction of children they allow no share, either of teaching or of discipline, to the ministers of the Church; and in many places they have procured that the education of youth shall be exclusively in the hands of laymen, and that nothing which treats of the most important and most holy duties of men to God shall be introduced into the instructions on morals."

In order to extirpate "this foul plague — *impuram hanc luem* — which is creeping through the veins of the State," the patriarchs, archbishops and bishops of the whole Church are urgently exhorted to "tear away the mask from Freemasonry," and let it be seen in its true colours. "By sermons and pastoral letters," they are "to instruct the people as to the artifices used by societies of this kind in seducing men and enticing them into their ranks, and as to the depravity of their opinions and the wickedness of their acts. As Our Predecessors have many times repeated, let no man think that he may for any reason whatsoever join the Masonic Sect, if he values his Catholic name and his eternal salvation as he ought to value them."

3

The struggle between anti-clericalism and Catholicism found expression in the "Fight for Rome" which was conducted with great obstinacy on both sides, which lasted for several decades, and has only been finally settled in our day. With the shots of the Italian cannon against the Porta Pia in the year 1870, Freemasonry and free-thought had forced their triumphant entry into the Eternal City; on the other hand, with every protest, with every anathema of Pius IX against this "robbery" and its perpetrators, the Papacy had inflexibly maintained its claim to temporal power over Rome.

So long as there existed the so-called "Roman Question," a deep and irreconcilable enmity reigned between the Vatican and the Quirinal, the residence chosen by Victor Emmanuel, the "Robber of the Papal States." This enmity between the two palaces on either side the Tiber did not cease even with death. When at the beginning of the year 1878, the King of Italy lay dying in the Quirinal, Pius, it is true, despatched a sacristan and a prelate to his rival's sick-bed to absolve him from the sentence of excommunication, but throughout the funeral solemnities for Victor Emmanuel, the bells of Rome remained silent at the Pope's command, and no higher ecclesiastic was allowed to follow the dead ruler to his last resting-place.

Hardly a month had passed when in the Vatican Pius closed his eyes forever. Again the two houses of mourning only took such notice of each other as the barest courtesy demanded: King Humbert sent his adjutant to the Camerlengo and bade him express his condolences. Not a single functionary of the Italian Government took part in the obsequies of the dead Pope.

On this question Leo XIII showed himself from the first moment of his elevation as unyielding as his predecessor. When, on his election, he had to impart his blessing to the people, he did this, not from the outer loggia of St. Peter's that looks out over the city, but from the inner one that looks into the Church itself; so that in this, the first public action of his pontificate, he pointedly turned his back on Italian Rome. Again, the accession of the new head of the Church was officially announced to all the governments of the world but not to the Government of the Kingdom of Italy on the other bank of the Tiber; and the Italian authorities took no official notice of the change of rulers at the Vatican. And in the same terms as his predecessor in the papal chair, Leo repudiated the Law of Guarantees which was put forward by Italy to govern the relations between the two powers.

It was Providence itself, the new Pope taught, that once assigned temporal sovereignty to the successor of Peter, and no rule of this world is older and more venerable than this, or has been "more legitimate in its origin, loftier and more worthy of respect in its aims"; how therefore can it be expected that in place of this sovereignty willed and consecrated by God, the Holy Father should express himself satisfied with an exterritoriality that is offered him like an alms by the hands of laymen? "The position which is supposed to be guaranteed to Us by law, is not one which befits Us and that We require; it is not a real independence, but only an apparent and transitory one, for it is subject to the will of others. This kind of independence can be taken away from Us again by him who gave it to Us; those who conferred it yesterday, can cancel it tomorrow."

The indispensable condition making it possible for the Vicar of Christ to be truly free and independent in the exercise of his office, consisted, as Leo unceasingly affirmed, in the full sovereignty and dominion of the Holy See over a piece of territory however small. As, however, the freedom of the head of the Church was at stake, the Roman question constituted, in contrast to the claims to sovereignty of temporal princes, not merely a matter of national and Italian interest, but a universal problem which affected all Catholics throughout the world, and which therefore should be solved in an international legal convention.

That Leo's attitude was bound up closely with his Thomistic theories is clear from one of his episcopal pastorals to his diocese of Perugia, wherein, long before he himself was called to the papal throne, he had tried to establish the claims of the Papacy to temporal sovereignty on the doctrine of the "hierarchy of ends" and on the graded organization of the universe as established by God. Without temporal dominion, he argued at that time, the Pope would be subject to whatever power was ruling the country; and therein lay a "subversion of ideas," a violation of the natural order of precedence in the world. "He who has to look after the highest end, cannot rationally be subordinate to those who work for inferior ends that only serve as means to the highest."

Proceeding therefore from the hierarchical world order of Aquinas, in which what is above the earth can never occupy lower rank than the earthly, Leo firmly adhered to the sovereign claims of the Papacy. With him it was not a question of the little strip of territory which was all that seemed to be at stake, but restoration of that great hierarchy in the universe, which through the violence offered to the Pope had become disordered and entangled at a vital point.

So during Leo's pontificate, the same insurmountable barriers were raised in the city of Rome and divided its society into camps of "Blacks" and "Whites." Those families who traditionally filled posts of honour at the papal court, ignored the royal court, and the chamberlains, ministers and officials of the king in their turn took no notice of the Vatican. No member of the "Black" nobility frequented a "White" house, and even the diplomatic representatives at the two courts had to adapt themselves to these unique usages.

A series of self-imposed embarrassments developed from this unnatural situation. Although there was nothing to prevent the Pope from leaving the Vatican when and as he pleased, nevertheless the whole of "Black" Rome held firmly to the thesis that the Vicar of Christ was a prisoner in his palace. On the other hand, the kingdom of Italy, in whose name the officials ruled the land, whose soldiers marched through the streets, whose flags fluttered from all the buildings, were regarded as non-existent by the papal party. For them the ruler in the Quirinal was now as before simply the "Duke of Savoy," and his new titles were held to have been illegally gained. From the "Duke of Savoy" the Pope might accept a present, to him he could send his blessing — but the "King of Italy" was officially unknown at the Vatican.

In such circumstances an event like the marriage of the heir to the throne, of the future King Victor Emmanuel III, must have created a series of insoluble difficulties of form. For dynastic reasons it seemed necessary that the ceremony should take place in Rome and according to Catholic rites; all the Roman churches however were directly under the Pope as bishop of Rome, and were therefore not accessible to members of the royal house. Finally an ingenious court official succeeded in discovering a small church which belonged not to the Pope but to the State. Having been built in the ruins of the palace of Diocletian, it had long been proclaimed a "national monument" and was therefore the property of the State. In this church the ceremony could at last take place.

The most complicated arrangements became necessary every time a foreign ruler appeared in Rome and wished to visit both the King of Italy and the Pope. Naturally etiquette demanded that the visiting sovereign should first of all pay his respects to the ruler of the land; the Vatican, however, obstinately refused to receive any one who visited the Pope second, for this would have to be regarded as a slight upon the Holy Father, as the inversion of the sole right order of precedence according to Catholic ideas. Accordingly during his sojourn in Rome the Emperor William II was compelled, on leaving the Quirinal, to proceed first of all to the Prussian Legation at the Vatican. Only from there, that is to say from Prussian soil, and in a Prussian royal carriage expressly procured from Berlin, could he betake himself to the Vatican, as though he were coming straight from his own home and not from the house of the enemy ruler.

On the state visit of King Alexander of Serbia, however, even this device failed, for Serbia at this time did not maintain a Vatican legation in Rome. So there was nothing to be done but for the Serbian minister in Berlin to come expressly to Rome and put up at a hotel, thereby stamping it as Serbian territory and creating a point of departure whence the king could drive to visit the

Pope and where Cardinal Rampolla could return his visit.

*
* *

"I am a stone," Pius IX had once said of himself, "where I fall, I lie." In this statement lay the admission of a lack of political talent. Pius accepted the situations into which his fate thrust him, and consequently he did not rise above the rôle of an irreconcilable.

Of Leo XIII, however, Gambetta, the anti-clerical Freemason and bitter opponent of everything Catholic, spoke on the day of his elevation in terms which expressed a high degree of admiration for the political talents of the new Pope: "The elegant and subtle Cardinal Pecci is elected. He is more diplomat than priest and thoroughly versed in all intrigues. He will not break with the traditions and with the pronouncements of his predecessor, but his demeanour, his conduct of affairs, will be more important than his speeches. And if he does not soon die, we may expect a marriage of convenience between the Church and the modern State."

And in fact the same man who had in his brief career as nuncio suffered so many failures, and who had then buried himself for several decades in the study of mediæval philosophy, now, as guide of the Church's destinies, became a true master of diplomacy. In his hands, the age-old and seemingly cumbrous and antiquated political machinery of the Vatican with its widely ramified net of official and secret agents and reporters, suddenly becomes again a vigorous and effective weapon of policy.

During the Kulturkampf Bismarck remarked that the

Pope was "a man who disposes of the consciences of two hundred million people" and was therefore "a mighty monarch." Pope Pius IX had for the most part asserted this power over two hundred million consciences only in negative resistance with his *"non possumus," "non expedit"* and such formulae, and had refused cooperation in the plans of secular governments. But Leo XIII understood how to use the Pope's authority over the Catholic world as a balance in the diplomatic game of the Powers, and so to give the "papal card" an unexpected value.

When Pius IX lay dying, hardly anyone save Bismarck and Dostoevsky realised what immense power the master of the Vatican still held in his hands. Under Leo, however, all the various governments began to recognize this, and before long they were vying with one another in their efforts to turn this power to the profit of their own plans and programmes.

Leo did not exhaust himself with threats and protests, but was ready to offer positive values to his partners in negotiation. For him the attitude of the Curia to the temporal powers of this world by no means appeared as something unequivocally fixed and ordained. He reserved to himself the right to use his influence with the Catholic masses freely in all directions, and was just as ready to support governments if they came to terms with him, as to attack them when they did not.

So the way was soon smoothed for that "marriage of convenience" between Rome and laicized France prophesied by Gambetta to which, on the morrow of the marriage, Leo brought with him for the French authorities a valuable dower: the reconciliation of the French Catholics with the Republic. Since the days of the French Revolution the Curia had always sympathized openly with the monarchical form of government

[109]

and regarded this form alone as approved by God. Now, however, Leo, taking his stand on the Thomistic distinction between primary and secondary causes, arrived at the conclusion that the form of government was not in itself a matter upon the value of which the Church was called upon to pronounce judgment. For the question involved was purely the earthly suitability of means to ends, a problem which every nation is competent to solve for itself according to the freedom of decision that belongs to it in the sphere of *causæ secundæ*. Accordingly, the Church, which has merely to safeguard the proper relation of the two orders of ends to one another, holds, Leo argued in his Encyclical *Sapientiæ christianæ*, that it is not her province "to decide which is the best among many diverse forms of government and the civil institutions of Christian States, and amid the various kinds of State rule she does not disapprove of any, provided the respect due to religion and the observance of good morals be upheld."

Quite clearly Leo separated himself from those French monarchists, who in their struggle against the Republic appealed to religious motives, since he declared in the same Encyclical that while "there can be no doubt but that in the sphere of politics ample matter may exist for legitimate difference of opinion, and that the single reserve being made of the rights of justice and truth, all may strive to bring into actual working the ideas they believe likely to be more conducive than others to the general welfare." Yet to "attempt to involve the Church in party strife, and seek to bring her support to bear against those who take opposite views," is to abuse religion, and is only worthy of partisans.

Shortly after Leo's Encyclical gave a theoretical basis to the recognition of the Republic by the Church, the French Cardinal Lavigerie, acting on the Pope's in-

structions, demonstrated its practical reality by a sensa
tional *démarche*. On the occasion of the visit of the
French fleet to the harbour of Algiers in the year 1890,
the Cardinal, amid the strains of the *Marseillaise*, gave an
address to the officers of the squadron in which he summoned all French Catholics to recognize and submit to
the form of government which the nation had now
finally accepted. Lavigerie concluded his speech with
a toast to the Republic, a gesture which aroused the
greatest indignation among French royalists but which
struck the rest of the world dumb with amazement.

The political gift which Leo, by this pointed repudiation of the monarchists, offered to the statesmen of the
Republic was sufficiently valuable to dispose the latter
to grant several concessions on their side. With the
aid of the Church the prospect was now opened to them
of restoring the internal unity of a country long torn by
party discussions, and of again raising France, still suffering from the crushing defeat of 1870, to the rank of
a Great Power capable of commanding respect abroad
and of contracting alliances with foreign powers.

Accordingly Gambetta declared that anti-clericalism
was not an "article of export," and that peace between
Church and State as between two equal and free Powers
appeared to him quite possible. In the year 1894 Spul-
ler, the Minister of Education and a special protégé of
Gambetta, expressly stated in a speech in the Chamber
that "a new spirit of tolerance, good-will, justice and
love" animated the government of the Republic in reli
gious questions.

*

* *

At the centre of Leo's diplomacy, however, stood
from the very beginning the "Roman Question." It

was primarily on this account that he sought to establish friendly relations with France and other foreign Powers, and that he favoured those currents among the Italian people which aimed at reconciliation with the Vatican. He hoped in this way gradually to isolate the Government of the Kingdom and, by bringing moral pressure to bear from without and from within, to compel it to yield to the wishes of the Holy See.

In the first years of his pontificate he actually did succeed in making the authorities of the Quirinal show a disposition to negotiate, for Italian government circles were beginning to feel all the difficulties and annoyances that the continued enmity of the Vatican and influential clergy brought in its train. The Vatican decree prohibiting Catholics from taking part in elections and from occupying posts in the administration of the country deprived both the Chamber and the machinery of government of a large body of highly acceptable citizens. The loyalty to the State of the Catholic population was permanently burdened with scruples of conscience, and the Government saw itself constantly confronted by a passive, yet none the less perceptible, opposition in home affairs which substantially weakened its position abroad.

So when Leo gave the Italian statesmen to understand that he was not averse to a reconciliation, Crispi himself, the convinced enemy of the Church, sought to reach an agreement with the Curia. Under the impression that with a man of Leo's type a settlement must be attainable, Crispi is said to have exclaimed: "Why cannot I discuss things directly with the Pope himself? How much we two would be able to clear up between us!"

In the 80's negotiations and conferences were carried on with the utmost secrecy through the medium of a Benedictine monk, and for a time things looked very promising. Indeed during this phase of Italo-Papal relations both parties made various gestures intended to prepare the public for the conclusion of peace. King Humbert had the tiara removed from his father's monument in Venice where it had originally been placed under the hoofs of the royal horse. On his journeys through the Italian provinces the king was received everywhere by the clergy with great marks of honour, and in Florence the archbishop embraced him before all the people and gave him his blessing. "This blessing, to which Leo XIII guided the archbishop's hand," wrote Father Tosti, the Librarian of the Vatican and one of the most zealous supporters of reconciliation, "came down as a dove with the olive-branch of peace upon the heads of the two Powers."

That these negotiations broke down just as their successful conclusion was expected on all sides is, according to Catholic writers, to be laid to the charge of the Masonic Lodge which forbade the Italian Ministers to make peace with the Curia. Liberal historians on the other hand ascribe the frustration of the work of reconciliation to the machinations of the Jesuits. They were accused of having used their influence with Leo to make him reassert the demand, which he had previously abandoned, for the restoration of papal sovereignty over the whole city of Rome, and in consequence of which the whole peace plan suffered shipwreck.

"After a period in which it was still hoped that a basis for reconciliation might be found," reports Iswolski, the Russian chargé d'affaires at the Vatican in the year 1889, to his Government in St. Petersburg, "we are now witnessing a renewal of the obstinate conflict between the administration of Signor Crispi and the more and more irreconcilable activities of the Vatican."

4

From the moment that the prospect of a peaceful settlement with Italy disappeared, Leo XIII began to prepare a way for the solution of the "Roman Question" along the paths of a widely extended foreign policy, the lines of which were carefully laid down with an eye to the future. This foreign policy, however, since it was directed to the restoration of the Papal States, had of necessity to be hostile to the Italian monarchy and to promote everything that might lower Italy's position in the world.

Leo had thought at first that he would be able to look for diplomatic support to the German Empire, a hope which the settlement of the Kulturkampf and the many marks of honour that had been paid him on the part of the German Government, seemed in some measure to encourage. Accordingly he used the occasion of the first visit to the Vatican of the young Emperor William II to make the latter a direct appeal, and to urge him to bring pressure to bear on Italy for the restitution of the papal territory.

In his reply, however, the Emperor, while emphasizing the "great glamour" that attached to the Papacy in the eyes of Europe, and declaring that "the name of Leo was enveloped in an aura of esteem and veneration," by no means showed himself prepared to make himself the agent of the Vatican as against Italy. On the contrary, the union between Italy and the Reich created by the Triple Alliance was strengthened at this very time and the House of Savoy found strong political support in Germany.

Austria, too, regarded in former times as the traditional protector of the Vatican, was now, through the Triple Alliance, compelled to take Italy into diplomatic consideration, and therefore declined to exert any sort of pressure on her allies in favour of papal interests.

It was as a direct result of these circumstances that the influence which Galimberti, the Germanophile nuncio at Vienna, had hitherto exercised on the political decisions of Leo, now suffered a marked decline. With the appointment of Mariano Rampolla as Secretary of State began that great change of Vatican policy which caused it to become the active and successful opponent of the Triple Alliance.

From now on the Pope and his Secretary of State "strove unceasingly (in the words of Iswolski) to extend the circle of their political relations as widely as possible, and to establish greater intimacy with those Powers which remained outside the closed compact."

By this time a new age of imperialism had reduced to a state of flux all solid combinations that had previously existed in the world of European politics, had burst old alliances and had removed old antagonisms. However in the formation of the new combination of Powers which led to the grouping that existed at the outbreak of the Great War, the influence of Leo XIII, though it did not appear on the surface, played a very important part. "A signal monument of suppleness, of penetration and of unerring judgment in regard to that regrouping of forces in Europe, of which only the first signs were as yet perceptible" is the verdict of a modern historian on the Vatican policy of that time.

By the effect of his Encyclical *Sapientiæ christianæ* on his dealings with the French Republic, Leo caused the same anti-clerical statesmen who had sent their soldiers against the monasteries to promise their secret support to the Vatican in its campaign for the restitution of the papal territory.

With Russia also, which was to become the ally of

France and the great opponent of the Triple Alliance, Leo paved the way for a new relationship. Like Great Britain, there was one point at which the Empire of the Czars was susceptible to the power of the Popes over Catholic humanity. If in the one case Ireland was the foreign body inside the religious and national unity of the State, here it was "Czarist Poland,"—a Catholic country in a state of constant unrest and always on the verge of rebellion, and possessing a population—which clung with fanatical faith to its clergy and allowed itself to be guided by them in every particular.

In St. Petersburg it was well known how greatly Catholic influence had contributed to the rebellious disposition of the Polish provinces. Yet hitherto the government had merely considered that the Roman clergy must be kept under strict survey as politically suspect and be deprived of all independence of action. The outbreak of the Polish revolt in the year 1863, however, gave a violent turn to the latent conflict between Russia and the Vatican. The Russian authorities now proceeded with vigour against the nationalist agitation of the Polish clergy, and Pius IX in return publicly asserted in his vehement way that the Czar was a schismatic and ruthless tyrant who was trying to stamp out Catholicism. In the course of the angry complaints which followed, the Russian chargé d'affaires in Rome told the Pope to his face that Catholicism was equivalent to revolution, and Pius thereupon showed him the door. After this painful incident in the year 1866, diplomatic relations between Russia and the Vatican had been broken off.

During the 80's the danger of a clash between Russia and Germany became an increasingly important factor in determining the course of the foreign policy of various cabinets, and with rare skill Leo at once contrived to utilize this situation for his own purposes. The coming war would have to be fought out on the soil of the old Polish kingdom partitioned between Prussia and Russia, and it might prove a matter of decisive military importance whether the Poles rose against Russia or whether they beheld a bitterer foe in Protestant Prussia and made common cause with the Russians. This depended in very considerable measure on the influence of the Catholic clergy upon the Polish people.

Leo now gave the Russian Foreign Minister Giers to understand that he might be prepared to use his influence with the Poles in a direction favourable to the Czarist Government, and again, as with France, the "papal card" won the game. Giers decided to enter into negotiations, and in the year 1888 he sent to Rome Alexander Petrowitch Iswolski, a young diplomat then at the beginning of a very promising career.

Although a Polish party at the Vatican did everything in its power to prevent the Pontiff from throwing his influence on the side of the Czarist régime, the Pope now sent instructions to the Polish bishops that they were to "impress upon the faithful the duty of obedience to the secular power and of docility towards the ruling authorities," and to see that no Catholic in Russia entered "any societies which are working for a revolution in the State or for the disturbance of peace and security." At the same time, the Curia did its utmost to cement the *rapprochement* between Russia and France and to dissipate the mistrust of the democratic Republic which still existed in conservative Petersburg.

Thus as in bygone centuries, the threads of world politics tended to meet at the Vatican, and Leo XIII realized one of his great ambitions. From the beginning it had been the aim of this Pope who, in the words of Iswolski, was "primarily a diplomatist and politician" to restore to the Papacy "its former international prestige and its influence upon the course of European events." This he had effectively accomplished.

With this development, there came about a change in the outward aspect which the papal residence offered to the world. In the lifetime of Pius IX, the Curia had quarrelled with practically all the Powers; one representative after another had been recalled from the Vatican, the ambassadorial palaces were deserted, and a wall of hostility had grown up round the papal throne. But now the Pope was again universally sought out and courted, and once again the Vatican Palace was the scene of stately receptions which for years past had been so rare as to be accounted curiosities.

Again foreign ambassadors and ministers drove up to the Court of St. Damasus in their horse-drawn state coaches, again the Swiss guard presented arms to princes, kings and emperors. Herr von Schlözer, the Prussian minister, and the French ambassador, Count Lefebvre, were the daily guests of the Cardinal Secretary-of-State Rampolla. Iswolski had arrived from far-off Petersburg, and the Duke of Norfolk appeared on official and secret missions from England, soon to be followed by a special envoy from Queen Victoria herself.

The Golden Jubilee of the Pope's priesthood saw representatives of almost all the sovereigns of Europe congregated at the Vatican. For this occasion even the Sultan of the infidel Turks and Caliph of all the Moslems sent one of his pashas to the court of the highest priest of Christendom.

*

* *

At first sight one is apt to find the political attitude of Leo XIII somewhat perplexing; it strikes one as incongruous, as full of contradictions. Sometimes, as in the case of the recognition of the French Republic, he seems to depart from all the traditions of the Curia; at others, as in the Roman Question, he holds rigidly to principles that appear obsolete. The same man who on every possible occasion extolled and honoured progress, who in his language assiduously cultivated a mild and conciliatory tone, employed against the Freemasons an altogether mediæval vocabulary of wrathful condemnation. Thus at one time he gave the impression of being almost a revolutionary innovator, at another seemed the obstinate defender of untenable anachronisms. Politicians like Gambetta and Iswolski saw in him a supple opportunist; men of the Church honoured him for his unswerving fidelity to principle and set him beside the figures of the great militant Popes of the Middle Ages. It is as if his character played from one colour into another, as if his activity oscillated between incompatible extremes.

Yet considered and judged in the light of its philosophical foundations, the policy of Leo in all its multiple facets is seen to be the logical expression of a complete system of ideas; and this system of ideas, from which all his actions, decisions and utterances proceeded and on the basis of which his political capacity and personality were shaped, is the "eternal philosophy" of St. Thomas.

These ideas justified his pact with the French Republic as well as his inflexible attitude towards Italy, they explained both his appreciation of cultural progress and his inability to appreciate the aims of Freemasonry. Moreover Leo could also appeal in a general way to Thomistic principles if, in dealing with the outside world, with which as guide of the Church's destinies he had to reckon, he did not despise political means and methods. His diplomatic adroitness, which has frequently been made a matter of reproach to him by critics of the severer sort as incompatible with his high spiritual office, was in reality nothing but the practical application of the knowledge that within the world the methods of the world are alone effective, and that only the proper utilization of these methods could bring about that success in the temporal sphere without which an actively functioning Church, whose very existence is closely bound up with earthly events, cannot possibly endure.

CHAPTER FIVE

RERUM NOVARUM

I

WHEN on the day following his election Leo entered the papal study for the first time, he found on the writing table among documents of many descriptions — among petitions from the Secretariat of Briefs, minutes of the Palatine Administration, of the Dataria and the Penitentiary, among reports of the Secretary of State, the Apostolic Camera and the Congregations — a letter addressed to the Holy Father, that had come through the post. This letter came from a certain Isaac Pereire, who stated therein that he was an old disciple of the doctrines of Saint-Simon and that he felt impelled to lay before the new Pope his views regarding the future mission of the Church.

It was true, Pereire argued, that although the new age was presenting itself in the guise of a secular development hostile to the Church, the Pope ought not on that account to lose sight of the fact that the ultimate aim of this universal revolution was the realization of ideas fundamentally Christian in character. The Church, which had at all times considered the protection of the suffering and oppressed as part of her mission, must now make the cause of the working class her own and place herself at the head of the social movement. Then might a truly Christian and just social order arise from the present ferment and confusion.

The confidence in Leo's far-sightedness manifested in this appeal from an unknown correspondent, together with the suggestion it conveyed that this Pope was called upon to effect the great work of directing the attention of the Church to the needs of the working classes, was to prove increasingly justified. For this great statesman in the Chair of Peter, who contrived to play his hand with such masterly skill in diplomatic affairs was not slow to recognize that in an era of imperialism social questions would drive all other problems into the background, and that an entirely new social duty now confronted the Church.

In this closing period of the nineteenth century when science and philosophy still clung to the liberal dogma of the "harmony of interests," when political economists and sociologists still sought to prove that the advantage of one necessarily involved the advantage of another, and that nothing should be done to interfere with the free play of economic forces, there were only two men, the Pope and Karl Marx, who perceived in all its significance the terrible and fateful reverse side of the great picture of industrial progress — that new and profound cleavage in the structure of society, splitting the human race into two hostile camps. Earlier in the 40's, these two men had watched simultaneously the rising growth of industrialism in the places where it was most developed, in Belgium, France and England: Joachim Pecci as nuncio of the Curia, Karl Marx as a hunted fugitive and revolutionary agitator. And both had seen that the same machinery to which modern society owed its unprecedented wealth, and by the help of which a small class of contractors and dealers amassed immense riches, had plunged millions of artisans into misery.

Leo and Marx describe these social conditions in the same language, with almost identical words. Like the revolutionary socialist, the supreme head of the Church points out in his Encyclicals how the concentration of control of means of production in the hands of a few individuals has brought it about that "a small number of very rich men have been able to lay upon the teeming masses of the labouring poor a yoke little better than that of slavery itself." The great majority of working men "have been surrendered, all isolated and helpless, to the hard-heartedness of employers and the greed of unchecked competition," and live in conditions of misery and degradation "repugnant to their dignity as human beings."

The result of civil change and revolution has been, says Leo, "to divide society into two widely differing castes." On the one side "there is the party which holds power because it holds wealth; which has in its grasp the whole of labour and trade; which manipulates for its own benefit and its own purposes all the sources of supply, and which is even represented in the councils of the State itself." On the other side "there is the needy and powerless multitude, down-trodden and suffering, and ever ready for disturbance." Accordingly Leo emphasized no less strongly than Marx the paramount importance of the rôle which belongs to the working class in the whole economic process of production, and which stands in such glaring contrast to the oppressed condition of this same working class. He recognizes that it is "only by the labour of workers that States grow rich," and it therefore seems to him a grave injustice that those persons who produce all the wealth should suffer want in the products of their own labour.

*

* *

But however much the two men agreed in their judgment of the social crisis, there was a fundamental difference separating them on all points where a programme of reform was concerned. From the moment that each turned aside from the contemplation of the situation to the investigation of its causes and the possibilities of its solution, there is apparent a profound opposition between their inherited philosophical views.

Marx, the devotee of rational analysis, whose thought was derived from Hegel and Feuerbach, fits the picture of the age into a mechanistic and dialectic world order which recognizes only the measurable and calculable forces of this material world, and fits every historical happening into the scheme of evolution and "progress." So viewed, the sharpening of class antagonism reveals itself as a necessary process: the increasing misery of the masses on the one side, the accumulation of wealth on the other — all is part of the evolution that conditions progress. The social crisis is a necessary phase of the process towards that logical climax which will bring about the dictatorship of the proletariat and ultimately a "classless society."

Dominated by this gloomy view of social ruin, Marx preaches class hatred and class war. Compared with the deep opposition between classes which is a social condition without remedy, all other lines of cleavage which can exist between man and man, appear to him of secondary importance. Differences of nationality, religion, language, race mean nothing as compared with the basic conflict between the exploiters and those exploited. All the capitalists of the world are arrayed on one great battle-front, on the other side stands the "proletariat of the world." What profits the one class spells ruin to the other, and so it has been since the beginning of time. This extreme accentuation of the social conflict should moreover be promoted by the proletariat and its leaders in every way possible, until the day arrives when the many shall rise and shake off the yoke which the few have laid upon them.

In opposition to this view, there reigned in the mind of the successor of Peter the concept of that universal order depicted by Thomas Aquinas, in which the natural and supernatural, human effort and divine ends, are harmoniously joined. One who like Leo sought a divine principle of order in the world, could not consider the evils of the capitalist system — which the Pope realized just as keenly as his Marxian opponent — as a necessary and logical stage in progress. On the contrary, the sharpening of the social conflict, the excessive enrichment of one class and the impoverishment of the other appeared to him as a departure by man from the original order designed by God, as a profound disorder, and as the corruption of the plan of creation caused by the failure and weakness of mankind.

The purpose and perfection of society is "to aim at and to attain the end for which it was formed." Hence to lose sight of this end, which according to Leo's philosophy could only be a metaphysical one, "implies disease, to go back to it, recovery." In Leo's view therefore the one and only way in which the world can be healed is by a change of heart; by a deliberate return to that great order which has its end in the metaphysical. It is a question of again humbly becoming part of this order, everyone in the natural place proper to him, so that an organic and harmoniously constituted society may arise again out of the distressing chaos.

*

* *

With the same clearness as the founder of modern Socialism, the Pope saw that in the masses of the proletariat the strongest power of the future was being formed, and that the coming age must belong to the one who understood how to win this new world power

for himself.   So Leo XIII resolved to take up the struggle for the soul of the working class and to carry the
action of Catholicism into the midst of the proletariat.

In her competition with Marxism the Church certainly seemed at the outset doomed to failure; for Socialist agitation had already worked profoundly on the
masses and filled them with contemptuous mistrust of all
representatives of religious principle.   To Marx, the
convinced materialist who regarded all events as exclusively generated and conditioned by material causes,
the doctrines of the Church concerning a divine and
spiritual power set above this temporal world were
bound to appear a snare and delusion.   He regarded
religion and belief in another life purely as an "ideological superstructure," as the expression of a definite economic phase.   The gods of antiquity like the God of
Christianity were simply reflections of the age-old
capitalist system.   The Ruler and Judge of heaven was,
he contended, nothing but an exact image of the earthly
exploiter, so that religion was simply the projection of
the prevailing social injustice into a hypothetical after-
life; it was therefore "the opium of the people," a de-
bilitating, paralysing narcotic whose effects were fatal.

In one of his writings Marx's friend and ally, Friedrich
Engels, formulated this conception with great force and
precision: "We want to clear out of the way everything
that proclaims itself to be supernatural and superhuman,
and thereby banish error; for the pretension of the
human and natural to be superhuman, supernatural, is
the root of all falseness and lies.   We have therefore
declared war once and for all upon religion and religious
ideas, and it matters little to us whether people call us
atheists or anything else."   Man, Engels goes on to say,
has only himself to think about, he must measure and
judge all life's circumstances solely in relation to him-

[126]

self, and "arrange the world on a truly human basis in accordance with the demands of his nature"; in this way alone will he solve "the riddle of our time. Not in future regions that have no existence, not above and beyond time and space, not in a God immanent in the world or set over against it, is truth to be found, but rather in the breast of man himself."

The churches of every confession were for Marxism simply tools of plutocracy, whose function it was to mobilize all the forces of superstition for the protection of the existing order and for the suppression of every movement of proletarian class consciousness. Accordingly the working class must count the Church among its irreconcilable enemies, and root out of its heart every stirring of religious belief that had been cunningly implanted there. Influenced by these views, the agitators of the new doctrine preached to the proletariat revolt from a Church which the Marxist August Bebel once described as the "greatest obscurantist institution in the world."

Moreover, many representatives of the clergy, mistrustful of social unrest and repelled by the revolutionary and atheistic character of Socialism, had condemned as sinful every demand for reform of the social order, and had thereby apparently confirmed the accusation of the Church's hostility to the workers. Those Catholic prelates, who like Archbishop Ketteler of Mainz or the English Cardinal Manning, had stood up boldly from the beginning for the rights of the working class, had met with violent opposition in their own camp and were even branded as "Socialists in disguise."

It was in the early years of Leo's pontificate, as he began to give his ideas practical shape, that the Marxian doctrine gained the upper hand among the working class all over Europe and supplanted the more moderate so-

[127]

cialist views that had hitherto prevailed. At the congresses of Marseilles, Ghent and Erfurt the Socialists dissociated themselves from the maxims of Proudhon, who had thought it possible to achieve the aims of the workers in a friendly arrangement with the capitalists, as well as from the national Socialism taught by Lassalle. "In every nation," ran one of these new resolutions, "let the disinherited class constitute itself into a great party, sharply marked off from all the bourgeois parties, and let this Socialist Party march hand in hand with the Socialist Parties of all other lands."

Thus was formed and organized that international proletariat which professed allegiance to no State and recognized no national frontiers, which beheld in every worker throughout the world a "comrade," in every capitalist a mortal enemy, and which, under the leadership of a group of fanatical intellectuals, worked systematically everywhere towards social revolution.

As early as the year 1878, Leo XIII had entered the lists against Socialism with his Encyclical *Quod apostolici muneris* in which he denounced the new movement in no unmeasured terms, characterizing it as "a deadly plague" which was tainting society to its very core. However, he soon felt the necessity of passing beyond such purely negative criticism. If he wished to combat Socialism with any prospect of success, he would have to oppose to the logically constructed programme of Marx — the triumph of which was largely due to its logical consistency — an equally complete, weighty and convincing conception of the social problem and its solution according to Catholic principles.

This task he attempted to fulfil in the Encyclical *Rerum novarum*, which the eighty-one-year-old pontiff gave to the world in 1891. The theoretical basis of this Encyclical is based on Thomism as are its practical conclusions and the ideal of society which Leo holds up to mankind as a goal worth the struggle.

2

"We approach the subject with confidence, and in the exercise of the rights which manifestly appertain to Us, for no practical solution of this question will be found apart from the intervention of religion and of the Church. It is We who are the chief guardian of religion and the chief dispenser of what pertains to the Church, and We must not by silence neglect the duty incumbent on Us."

These lofty words, with which the Encyclical *Rerum novarum* passes from a general survey of the conditions of the time and from a criticism of Socialism to the presentation of the Catholic programme, characterize the spiritual attitude from which Leo approaches the problem. The things of earth, he continues, "cannot be understood or valued aright without considering life to come, the life that will know no death." If we disregard this then "the whole scheme of the universe becomes a dark and unfathomable mystery."

If, however, we start from the "life to come," then man, who in the conception of Marxist materialism is nothing more than a "nexus of economic relations," becomes in the divine plan of creation a member endowed with the fullest personal dignity. Every human creature, be he ever so poor and lowly, is stamped with the seal of God, and so possesses a dignity which "no man may outrage with impunity"; indeed God Himself has ennobled all his creatures in that He has destined them to co-operate in His divine plan.

Seen in the light of this plan, society, like the rest of creation, is a gradated order consisting of various ranks and stations. Here Leo comes into sharp conflict with

[129]

the theory of equality which from the days of the Enlightenment had governed all democratic programmes and had finally been incorporated into Socialism. For whereas the purely material outlook infers merely from the external agreement that appertains to members of the species, the legal equality of everything that "wears a human countenance," and ultimately raises the demand for the removal of material inequalities, Thomism beholds humanity as an infinite multiplicity of different "natural states," dispositions and vocations.

The equality of all before God, which Christianity has taught from the beginning, by no means removes, says Leo, the difference in capacities, fortune, rights and authority, which likewise has its source in God. This unequal condition of things human must be endured. "No matter what changes may occur in forms of government, there will ever be differences and inequalities of condition in the State. Society cannot exist or be conceived of without them." The aim of the Socialists, therefore, "to reduce civil society to one dead level" is a vain striving against nature.

"He who has created and governs all things," Leo had already written in his earlier Encyclical *Quod apostolici muneris*, "has in His provident wisdom so disposed them that the lowest attain to their end by the middlemost, and the middlemost by the highest. Just then as the Almighty willed that, in the heavenly kingdom itself, the choirs of angels should be of differing ranks, subordinated the one to the other; again, just as in the Church God has established different grades of orders with diversity of functions, so that all should not be *apostles, all not doctors, all not Prophets;* so also has He established in civil society many orders of varying dignity, right and power. And this to the end that the State, like the Church, should form one body comprising many members, some excelling others in rank and importance, but all alike necessary to one another and solicitous for the common welfare."

The principle of order also determines man's relationship to the material goods of the world. As man is called by his destiny to rule over all creation, never may he be made subject to anything that belongs to the sphere of things. Therefore "it is shameful and inhuman to treat men like chattels to make money by, or to look upon them merely as so much muscle or physical power." For greedy speculators to exploit the indigent and the destitute for the sake of gain and to gather profit from the work of another, is condemned by all laws, human and divine. For by such conduct man is degraded from the lofty plane of the dignity due to him to a lower state of oppression and thralldom which is not proper to him.

It is as God's creature endowed with the dignity of moral freedom that man stands against the world, and this indestructible freedom and personality also ennobles and sanctifies every labour performed by man. Whereas both Liberalism and Marxism had separated labour from the person of the labourer and regarded it as a political and economic factor, as a commodity on the market of supply and demand, the Pope points to the indissoluble connection between the individual and the work he performs: "Labour is personal, inasmuch as the exertion of individual strength belongs to the individual who puts it forth and who employs such strength to procure that personal advantage on account of which it was bestowed."

Labour therefore can never be sold, can never become a commercial commodity, never have a price. All labour is creative effort, and in so far as it is performed in harmony with the universal scheme of things, it is accomplishing the work of divine Providence; through it man becomes God's collaborator.

While labour thus takes rank among the ends of humanity, wealth preserves only the character and value of a means. Certainly Leo condemns in the strongest terms the Socialist programme, which aims at doing away with private property. Such endeavours are only calculated to "incite the poor man's envy of the rich" and are absolutely powerless to solve the social problem. On the contrary the working class itself would be the first to suffer if the Socialist remedies were put into effect, and such remedies, moreover, are "emphatically unjust, because they would rob the lawful possessor, bring State action into a sphere not within its competence, and create utter confusion in the community."

At the same time, however, though the unequal possession of property seems justified by the inequality of states and callings, yet wealth and power are never blessings for their own sake, nor may those who possess them dispose of them just as they please, as if they were their very own. They have been lent to man as "adjuvamina," in order that he may use them aright and in conformity with the plan of creation. "Whoever has received from the Divine bounty a large share of temporal blessings, whether they be external and corporeal, or gifts of the mind, has received them for the purpose of using them for the perfecting of his own nature, and at the same time, that he may employ them, as the steward of God's Providence, for the benefit of others."

For right possession and right use are two different things. Private ownership "is the natural right of man," and the exercise of that right is both lawful and necessary. But for the right use of one's possessions it is necessary "to give to the indigent out of what remains over" when one's own needs have been supplied.

[132]

The rich man therefore must help the poor man. He stands towards him in a relationship of obligation. The assistance he proffers him is not an alms, which he can give or refuse according to his mood; on the contrary the rich man is in duty bound to allow the poor man to share his surplus wealth, for precisely the higher social standing of the rich man also lays upon him a higher social responsibility. He in turn whose destiny has placed him in a subordinate position in the community has likewise a duty to the corporate whole, and must fulfil to the best of his abilities the task assigned to him in that station.

In Leo's view therefore it is a great mistake to assume that "class is naturally hostile to class, and that the wealthy and the working men are intended by nature to live in mutual conflict." Actually the direct contrary is the truth, for it is of the very nature of society that "all groups should, as it were, groove into one another, so as to maintain the balance of the body politic."

In place of the Marxian conception of class, which in its very formulation establishes the opposition of one class to another, the papal Encyclical returns to the Thomistic conception of "orders" which grade into one another upwards and downwards, all working harmoniously for a higher common end.

In this order every human activity from the lowest occupation to the highest finds its place in a hierarchical scale of "offices"; here there is no meaningless collision of mutually antagonistic forces in a conflict of self-interests, but a cooperation of all in the service of a common destiny beyond this material universe.

Just as the individual man in his social conduct is bound by ethical principles, so too is the State, for on it lies the duty in the great hierarchy of the world, of seeing that the moral law is observed within the societies under its control. Hence the State may by no means regard itself merely as the legal protector of the propertied classes, "since it is the province of the State to consult the common good." It must therefore "duly and solicitously provide for the welfare and the comfort of the working classes; otherwise that law of justice will be violated which ordains that each man shall have his due." Indeed the very conception of a State organization involves the partnership of "high and low." The poor "are members of the national community equally with the rich," and it would be "irrational to neglect one portion of the citizens and favour another."

Certainly it behooves the State to safeguard the rights of property and to prevent violence and disorder. But where social unrest is caused by real evils, the government should intervene to remove these causes in good time, and to see that the workers obtain their rights. It will always be the duty of the authorities to save the lower orders from "the cruelty of greedy speculators, who use human beings as mere instruments for money-making." For the State exists "to protect natural rights, not to destroy them."

The concluding section of the Encyclical *Rerum novarum*, in which the forming of Catholic workingmen's associations is recommended, culminates in the statement that "the condition of the working classes is the pressing question of the hour," and that on its right solution hangs the welfare of the whole of society. This solution Christian workingmen will easily find "if they will form associations and choose wise guides."

3

Whereas the thought of the age, preoccupied with earthly affairs, is fixed solely on the distribution of material wealth and sees in this the only way to the attainment of human happiness, Leo in his social pronouncements always returned to the immaterial values of existence, to moral virtue and perfection. He insisted that it is only pride, which in the last analysis causes dissensions among men, while insight into the superiority of moral over material blessings dispels this pride and, in the common striving of all after that "highest good" which can alone "make either men or angels perfectly happy," restores the social harmony. "We know that the blessings of nature and the gifts of grace belong to the whole human race in common, and that from none except the unworthy is withheld the inheritance of the Kingdom of Heaven."

It is Christian wisdom therefore which defines the nature of all rights and duties, and all strife would quickly cease were society to follow this wise guidance. Then each individual would find his fitting condition in the great order of obligations ; what he accomplished therein would always be related to the common good, and a profound solidarity would bind together all members of the social community.

With this ordination of the social problem to metaphysical values, Leo again introduced ethical principles into the consideration of social and economic questions, from which, since the doctrines of Adam Smith, Ricardo and other exponents of the independence of the economic law, they had been banished. Now Leo in his turn, as Thomas had once done, judged men's actions in their economic life by the principles of morality and thereby transformed problems of power into problems of right. Indeed he was convinced that only by strictly adhering to the moral law is it possible to draw rich and poor, employer and employee together, and to place their respective rights and duties on an equitable basis.

It goes without saying that the bold and idealistic attempt of this Pope, in the midst of a materialistic and scientific age, to place the study of the social question on a metaphysical basis, and in this way to hold out new possibilities for its solution, made a profound impression on the world of the latter nineteenth century, and occasioned no little amazement in many quarters.

True; the Encyclical *Rerum novarum* was greeted with derision by the Socialist leaders like every other pronouncement of the Church; but the working class learned from the pulpit and in Catholic debating clubs, not without surprise, that this Pope spoke a language which evinced understanding and sympathy for their condition, that the rights of the proletariat were recognized, the injustices of the capitalist system sharply criticised, the efforts of the workers to organize themselves warmly encouraged. Thus the papal Encyclical proved at once an invaluable aid to those men who had been endeavouring for a long time to build up a Catholic workingmen's movement.

"Who can describe," wrote one of these Catholic organizers, the Count de Mun, "the astonishment, the general enthusiasm, the fervent prayers of thanksgiving that this Encyclical aroused in the hearts of all! Ideas that until yesterday had been stigmatised as subversive and pernicious are today sanctioned by the highest authority in the world. Imagine the stir in doctrinary circles and the even greater excitement among the workers, who had been warned time after time that they had nothing to expect from Rome but the punitive arm of the head of the Church raised in excommunication! And now they see how he stretches out his hand to them like a father to bless them!"

In this deliverance of Catholic social effort from its manifold doubts and hindrances lay the immediate practical significance of the papal pronouncement. It had as its result that thenceforward a Catholic mass movement opposed itself with ever increasing strength to Marxian agitation. It was no longer necessary to regard Marxism as the only way to the solution of the social question. Against it there now stood a second conception to which all those people could adhere who were striving to find a remedy for the ills of society, but who were too deeply imbued with the spirit of religion to be able to identify themselves with the Socialist programme.

Thereafter Leo did his utmost to foster the growth of this Catholic social movement, and in one pronouncement after another he pointed out that it lay with the workers themselves to build up a new society, and that it was the duty of the Church to assist them in every possible way. For the working class was, he declared, "a true member in the organism of the State" and lived its own cultural life which it had a right to develop to the full.

Hence the English sociologist Devas, in a study on the influence exerted by Leo on his time, writes that as in former epochs of history the Church had been described as "the Church of the catacombs," "the Church of the Fathers," and "the Church of the Middle Ages," so the period of Leo XIII could best be characterized as "the Church of the people."

The Pope himself in a letter to the General of the Order of Friars Minor made use of the phrase: "More than ever is it the people upon whom the welfare of the State chiefly depends"; and a few years before his death he exhorted the French bishops: "Go among the people! Go to the workers! Go to the poor!"

In the Encyclical *Graves de commune*, promulgated in the year 1901, Leo returned once again to social questions and protested anew against the assumption that this was purely an economic problem: "The precise opposite is the truth, that it is first of all moral and religious, and for that reason its solution is to be expected mainly from the moral law and the pronouncements of religion."

"How important it is," exclaimed the ninety-year-old Pope, in an address to the clergy, "to go among the people and work for their welfare!" As a result of such social activity on the part of the Church, Leo hoped that the masses would once again find themselves to be Christian men, and "freely fulfilling the obligations of virtue and religion, strive to attain that final good for which we came into the world." And when once they "throw their mighty will into the scale of world events," a new, transformed society will arise, which "will count it an honour to bend its knee before God."

CHAPTER SIX

QUADRAGESIMO ANNO

I

THE Year One of the Christian dispensation was not followed by an age in which earth, become Paradise again, bore a transfigured and redeemed humanity on her course among the planets. No matter how frequently in subsequent times saints, heroes and rescuers from misery here and there gave their lives, performed great deeds, expounded ideas, thought out philosophic systems, and created institutions, their efforts to bring about the welfare of humanity never led to that terrestrial harmony which was so ardently desired and so often seemingly just within reach. History has moved relentlessly onward, ever disavowing with cynical brutality every sacrifice, every effort, every program of action that was to bring about the millennium.

And yet the deep inner wisdom of mankind recognizes not the success but the superhuman undertaking and even its tragic failure as true greatness. Reverence and admiration often transfigure the memory of such men as have been broken, betrayed, deserted, and have suffered shipwreck of all their hopes. The figure of that ruler and conqueror who set out to unite Europe with the sword and who ended his days as a prisoner at St. Helena has grown into a legend.

Whenever the historical judgment of the world begins to weigh and evaluate, it is guided by the loftiness of the aim, by the magnitude of the struggle in which warriors, thinkers and reformers have cast their spiritual forces. Such a standard of measurement at once brings out the essential greatness of St. Thomas and of his Papal Disciple of the nineteenth century, of those two minds which boldly set for themselves the task of bringing into accord faith and reason, religious and secular life. The superficial appraisal which is guided merely by success may not see beyond their practical failure, and on shallow evidence may point to the fact that neither St. Thomas nor Pope Leo succeeded finally in solving the contradiction between faith and reason, the Church and the world, that even today this contradiction still evokes deep discord among men.

But what in the Middle Ages finally wrecked the work of St. Thomas and in our own time militates against the success of the Leonine programme, is the desire for rationally certain, demonstrable knowledge, proof against all doubt; and inherent in this desire is a mighty force which has acted as a determining factor in our whole spiritual culture, yes, in the very life and constitutions of European States. The attempt, however, to bring these powerful aspirations of rational thought into harmony with the opposing philosophy founded on faith in the supernatural and weld them into a single system, must be deemed an aim of such sweeping grandeur that practical failure cannot dim the pure lustre of the undertaking.

*
*   *

Thomas Aquinas passed away at the beginning of the year 1274 in the Cistercian monastery of Fossanuova, where illness had overtaken him on the journey to the Council of Lyons. He died in the firm conviction that he had united for all time reason and divine contemplation, the natural and the supernatural, in an order of ends ascending to God; indeed, of his great *Summa* embracing all creation, only the third part, devoted to the redemptive work of Christ, remained unfinished.

It soon became manifest, however, that what St. Thomas had built into the structure of Christian theology had been merely the Aristotelian form of rational thought, but not the desire for rational knowledge itself. And in the centuries that followed it was precisely this Aristotelianism that was discarded by rationalism, refusing to remain satisfied any longer with the methods and deductions of the Stagirite. To the sceptical mind of the dawning modern era, both the methods by which the Greek philosopher arrived at his conclusions and the assumptions from which he proceeded began to appear more and more debatable. Soon there was called into question that very order of ideas upon which Thomas had based his synthesis: the doctrine of entelechies, of the ordination of all being and thinking to higher, supernatural ends.

In the young nobleman René Descartes, who while a pupil of the Jesuit college of La Flèche had been taught that *ratio* and *fides* had been united for all time by the philosophies of Aristotle and Thomas, the unconquerable doubt, which refused to be longer satisfied with the solutions of Aristotelianism, gained complete ascendency. To him the logic of the Stagirite in its attempt to reach the transcendental lacked freedom and betrayed an obvious bias; for with all its display of syllogistic deductions, it never did more than try to prove an *a priori* assumption. Accordingly, to the inductive method of Aristotle and of the Thomistic philosophy that rested upon it, Descartes opposed his principle of unprejudiced thinking and of inevitable doubt to the last.

At about the same time a similar revolt against Aristotelianism broke out in all departments of European intellectual life. Wherever philosophers devised new systems, wherever investigators explored the secrets of nature, they came to the conclusion that the Thomistic-Aristotelian belief in a principle of ends and forms governing creation constituted the chief source of all prevailing errors and confusion.

A short while after Giordano Bruno had suffered at the stake for his daring protest against Aristotelian philosophical principles, the learned Lord Chancellor Bacon of Verulam, when not engaged in affairs of state and the business of political corruption, sat in London composing philosophical and scientific treatises in which with biting sarcasm he combated the Stagirite's belief in final causes and covered the whole theory with ridicule. Possessing as he did the purely scientific type of mind which sought knowledge not by philosophical speculation but by the actual investigation of perceptible natural processes, to him the search for final causes and ends in nature seemed "barren and fruitless." In his opinion Greek philosophy before Aristotle, when it was still unhampered by the idea of final causes (the natural philosophy of a Democritus, or an Anaxagoras), had been "more real and better inquired" than that of the Stagirite, for the reason that it "did not suppose a mind or reason in the frame of things, but attributed the form thereof . . . to infinite essays or proofs of nature" and assigned the particularities of causes to the necessity of matter, without intermixture of final causes.

It was at such a science "without intermixture of final causes" that Bacon and his age now aimed. They sought an insight into natural occurrences which acquired its certainty from actual observation that could be tested at any time, and not from previously assumed "entelechies" that lacked conclusive proof.

Hence as compared with Aristotelianism, a fundamental change took place in the way scientific enquiry approached its material. Bacon expressly repudiated the view that it is the task of science to discover the first causes and final ends of the sensible world; on the contrary what have to be explored are simply the "secondary causes" at work in each case, that is to say, the causative links connecting an occurrence with one that immediately preceded it. But the idols of teleology which the human mind has worshipped for so long, "must be abjured and renounced with firm and solemn resolution" in order that the dominion of man over the world with its forces and riches might begin.

With even greater precision Galileo defined the mission of the new science, declaring that this is never concerned with the "why" but only with the "how." When the investigator examines a particular phenomenon, his task is accomplished the moment he has established all the measurable factors of the case and brought them into an externally valid relation with one another; he need not concern himself in the slightest degree with the "final cause" or "end" of the occurrence.

Thus the transcendental "contemplation of being," which formed the content of Aristotelian and Thomistic speculation, gave place to the search for a natural law that could be apprehended mathematically and tested and proved by experiment. The world of perceived things, from which all "entelechies" have been discarded, became a mechanical interplay of material objects whose workings were of measurable dimensions and capable of quantitative definition.

For a Europe whose mode of thought and life was thus transformed, the once greatly admired "philosopher" and his renovator, Thomas, soon lost all glamour. What had once been revered as sacred knowledge, now passed for barren, worthless theorizing upon questionable assumptions incapable of solid proof. Bacon indeed described the whole Aristotelian philosophy as "the childhood of science, fertile in controversy, barren of effect," as "unemployed capital" which could yield no profits. For centuries past this science had, to his way of thinking, produced nothing but idle disputations which only served to obscure the problems they were supposed to solve. "The whole tradition and succession of instructions exhibits as on a stage the characters of master and scholar, but not that of the inventor, or of him who has added anything excellent to inventions."

So completely was the Thomistic-Aristotelian system supplanted by the new order of philosophy and natural science, that the sale of Aristotle's work practically ceased after the seventeenth century. It came about finally that such thinkers as Schopenhauer thought they could brush aside all scholastic philosophy as an incomprehensible aberration of the human mind.

From the end of the Middle Ages to the present time, European thought has been a work destroying the foundations of Aristotelianism and consequently of Thomism. Not only spiritually, but politically and economically as well, the world has undergone during this period a greater transformation than ever before in its history, and in this process it had learned to free itself in every respect from the consideration of "higher ends" and to adapt itself exclusively to temporal interests.

But, unruffled by all these changes, the Catholic Church has clung faithfully to the system of St. Thomas and preserved it as a precious treasure throughout centuries dominated by quite alien intellectual trends. The death of Aquinas was mourned by the whole Christian world; he was termed in obituary notices and memorials of the time the "Angelic Doctor" and the "brightest of stars"; and soon the theology of the Middle Ages was accepting, in conformity with his views, the "handmaid of reason," thitherto so much feared, as the servant of faith. The heathen Aristotle could now make his entry unopposed into the philosophy of Christendom.

Even in the days when the Age of Enlightenment (so called) was dawning, the Jesuits, who had become the most zealous advocates of Thomistic Aristotelianism, prescribed that their educational institutions must abide by the principle that philosophy and natural science were to be taught "not merely in accord with truth, but also in the Aristotelian sense," and that no teacher was to abandon "in matters of any importance" the method of Thomas and the Stagirite. Thus was the *philosophia perennis* of Thomas handed down from generation to generation to the time of Leo who once again brought it into living touch with the realities of life.

*
* *

On July 3, 1903, the aged Pontiff Leo XIII returned from a drive in the Vatican gardens tired and feverish and had to betake himself to bed. The doctors diagnosed pulmonary congestion and pronounced his condition grave. In the morning of that same day the Pope had corrected proofs of his Latin poem on Anselm of Canterbury and had worked with his private chaplain on the despatch of important papers. Toward evening he was to receive the Viaticum, the Sacrament for the dying with which every good Catholic is prepared for the last journey. It was administered to him by his confessor, at the head of a solemn procession, after Leo himself had recited the *"Confiteor Deo omnipotenti. . ."* At the same time the Blessed Sacrament was exposed in

[145]

all the churches of Rome, and the faithful throughout the world prayed for the stricken Pontiff.

His body, now a mere shadow, fought against the power of death. He continued to carry on animated discussions with the French cardinals about religious conditions in their country, with Cardinal Rampolla about political problems, with the doctors about his health. On July 20, however, he declared his hour had come, and while in hundreds and thousands the people of Rome crowded before the Vatican, he bade farewell to the cardinals and prelates who surrounded his couch. At 4 o'clock in the afternoon he gave up the ghost; his age was ninety-three years and four months.

Now the Camerlengo had his duties to perform. At his command the gates of the Vatican were closed, and the penitentiaries of St. Peter's took up their watch, reciting the prescribed prayers for the dead. The Camerlengo formally announced the death of the Pope; solemnly the Fisherman's ring of Leo XIII was broken.

During the following night two chaplains transferred the urn containing the dead man's heart to the church of SS. Vincent and Anastasius; his body clothed in the white talar and arrayed with dalmatic, pallium, gold mitre and ivory cross, was escorted by cardinals, bishops, court officials and members of the diplomatic corps, to the Vatican Basilica, where from the early hours of the following morning the people were allowed to file past the remains.

When the eyes of Leo XIII were sealed by death, there was lost the vision of a cosmos in which all things, ordered in spheres and ascending hierarchies, course round Divine splendour in eternal harmony. When the body of this old man of ninety-three was laid to rest, there vanished from the midst of men a spirit also which had finally absorbed everything fleshly and become

[146]

purest, keenest thought. That spirit, while housed in the brain now cold, had resolutely felt its way into the ultimate mysteries of that great, all-embracing system of thought in which reason is merged in the divine vision, the natural in the supernatural, the state in the Church, and the earth in heaven. Leo alone had grasped its indissoluble totality. Likewise the instant which marked the coming of everlasting silence to the lips of this Pope recorded the passing of the magic spell of that supple, diplomatic speech with which he had always managed to bring his adversaries under his influence, inducing them to make concessions and compromises and to conjoin their mundane interests with the metaphysical demands of the Church.

Temporarily the vision which had absorbed him was kept aglow by the chorus of praise which, in the form of panegyric, was sung in every part of the world over his grave. For a time the universal order which his thought had pieced together still cohered, and the magic spell which had been cast by his utterance continued to exert its power. But in everyday mundane reality, nothing could halt the dissolution of the cosmos into disorder and dissonance, however incompatible these were with what was said in Leo's praise. The ancient opposites of reason and the insight of faith, of natural and supernatural, of earth and Heaven, returned. Once more that inharmoniousness was there, from which only the glance of this one man, so long as it was not dimmed, had redeemed the world so that it became a great unity, a system, a harmony. Such was the power of his spirit until it went to its reward, and the might of his voice while it had not yet died away.

Barely had he, the conciliator, been carried to his grave, when thought sundered itself from belief, what is from what ought to be, the State from the Church.

The Popes who followed Leo once again confronted a world surrendered unto atomic individualism and dissonance. They found themselves on a battlefield where the eternal Church must be defended anew against a besieging world.

*

* *

As Leo's successor assumed office laicized France was preparing herself to shake off those ties formed by Leo which had bound her to the higher order of the Church. The peace policy which Leo had always pursued with particular zeal towards "the eldest daughter of the Church" was in ruins; the opposition between laicism and Catholic principles proved too much in the long run for the arts of Leonine diplomacy, and so the "marriage of convenience" between State and Church came to an abrupt end a few years after it had been contracted. For with a conviction just as earnest as that inspiring the champions of Catholicism, millions of Frenchmen regarded the secular philosophy of "enlightened" reason as a living faith, and strove for its universal adoption. Thus the *idée laïque*, in spite of temporary currents moving in other directions, always reasserted itself afresh as the dominant power in the State.

An event provocative of public feeling like the Dreyfus affair was sufficient to cause barely restrained antagonism to break out anew. At the turn of the century all advocates for the revision of the Dreyfus case formed themselves into an anti-clerical alliance, headed by politicians like Clémenceau, authors like Anatole France, scholars like Ernest Lavisse. "To be *laïc* means to refuse to place reason under the yoke of dogma, not to admit that the spirit of man must retire before the incomprehensible."

[148]

The anti-clerical laws which placed the whole clergy of France under strict government control followed one another in rapid succession. In the year 1904 the French ambassador was recalled from the Vatican, and in 1905 the Paris Chamber decided upon the complete separation of Church and State. Even the Catholic social movement which Leo had promoted with such zeal and in which he had seen the way to a truly Christian harmony of social relations, threatened under his successor to break loose from the hierarchical structure and to emancipate itself from the Church's guidance.

In France it was the movement of the "Sillon," founded by Marc Sangnier, which, in its endeavours to realize republican and socialistic ideas in a Catholic spirit, now aroused misgivings. The new Pope had to administer to it a sharp rebuke for "obstinately withdrawing itself from the direction of those deputed by heaven to guide individuals and societies in the path of truth and well-being." Indeed, the whole "Sillon," once one of the hopes of Catholic social work, now appeared to the Vatican as a "wretched tributary of the great movement of organized apostasy in all countries, which aims at erecting a universal Church without dogma or hierarchy, without rules for the spirit or reins for the passions."

In the same first decade of the twentieth century there also sprung up in Italy under the leadership of the Catholic priest Romolo Murri an "autonomous movement" which refused to allow the Papal See and the episcopate any influence upon the decision of Catholics in the practical affairs of civil life, but proposed, on the contrary, to conduct a plan of social action on the basis of its own authority alone.

The tendency to break loose from supernatural ties penetrated even into the seminaries and threatened to

[149]

infect the clergy with its dangerous spirit; indeed, anxious rectors and superiors had to report that lithographed pamphlets containing essays on the Kantian philosophy and other critical and unorthodox doctrines were being secretly circulated among their pupils, and that these pernicious writings had exercised a deep influence upon the impressionable minds of future clerics.

2

The general onslaught of these emancipatory ideas compelled the Church, after the death of the conciliator-Pope Leo, to fall back on her own forces, and to organize them anew in a period of intense inward concentration.

The College of Cardinals which assembled in Conclave on July 31, 1903, drew from the existing situation the conclusion that the new head of the Church should be a man of an essentially different type from his predecessor. It may well be that external circumstances, like the veto of the Emperor Franz Joseph against Cardinal Rampolla, the enemy of the Triple Alliance, may have contributed to the result of this papal election; but certain it is that it was a deeper feeling for the needs of the Church at the time that finally determined the electoral college not to choose as Pope the adroit Rampolla, Leo's Secretary of State and close collaborator, the man whose whole activity had been directed to the end of realizing Leo's vision of the great harmony in practical politics. Instead the Conclave elected the pious and unworldly Patriarch of Venice, Joseph Melchior Sarto, a man wholly absorbed in the affairs of religion and little conversant with the ways of the world.

Son of a village tailor, Sarto gradually rose from a simple seminarist to ever higher offices in the priestly calling: he successively filled the posts of canon, chancellor, synodal examiner, bishop, archbishop and cardinal, until finally the tiara was placed upon his head. The man who now took the name of Pius X had never busied himself with politics, standing aloof from Vatican diplomacy, and had always devoted himself solely to the care and reform of the dioceses placed under him. Accordingly he began his pontificate with a programme which disregarded politics entirely and sought salvation only in the inner forces of the Church. From the first the new Pope declared that his aim was to restore all things in Christ—*"instaurare omnia in Christo."*

If in his earlier career and as head of the Church he achieved practical success in his dealings with the powers of the world, he obtained it, not as Leo had done, with the polished weapons of statecraft, but by a simple directness of character. When he was Patriarch of Venice he had been led on sudden impulse to seek out the king of Italy and to explain to him frankly the disadvantages of the tension that existed between the political and ecclesiastical authorities in his diocese, and he had obtained a prompt removal of his grievance.

This same simple directness caused him, immediately on his election, and at the mere request of one of his Noble Guard, to turn his steps towards the outer loggia of St. Peter's to bestow his blessing from this point. He was only persuaded to give up the idea when it was pointed out to him that such a course would be interpreted as too significant a gesture of reconciliation towards Italy.

As a son of the people he considered as injurious to their interests the virtual disfranchisement of Italian Catholics resulting from the instructions issued to them by his predecessors not to take part in elections, and he modified very considerably the decree forbidding them to participate in the political life of the country. This

[151]

again did much to promote better relations between the two powers.

But apart from such occasional outbursts of his impetuous temperament, the pontificate of Pius X is notable as a period of stern and vehement resistance to those secular forces which were working again with renewed violence to nullify the work of reconciliation undertaken by Leo, to estrange mankind from Catholicism and to attack the Church at her very roots.

Like Pius IX, from whom he took his name, Pius X raised his voice in angry protest to the world. When he formally broke with infidel France he justified this step by the declaration that he could not do otherwise without breaking the oath he took on ascending the Chair of Peter and without imperilling the Church.

"We await without fear the verdict of history. It will say that with our eyes fixed immovably on the higher rights of God which we have to defend, we have not sought to humiliate the civil power or to combat a form of government, but to safeguard the inviolable work of our Lord and Master Jesus Christ. It will say that what we have claimed and claim for the Church of which the Church of France is the oldest daughter and an integral part, is respect for her hierarchy, the inviolability of her property, and her liberty; that if Our request had been listened to, religious peace in France would not have been disturbed, and that on the day on which this request is listened to, the peace that is so greatly to be desired will return."

No less energetically did Pius X proceed against the rebellious tendencies that were manifesting themselves in Catholicism itself. In regard to the "autonomous movement" within the Italian social unions, he pointed out that all Catholic organizations are strictly obliged to carry out their programmes "in dependence upon the ecclesiastical authorities, in complete submission and obedience to the bishops and their representatives." Upon Murri, the leader of the "autonomists," who refused to submit to these regulations, Pius finally pronounced sentence of excommunication.

The news that "modernist" views were gaining ground in the seminaries and universities induced Pius X to issue, like Pius IX, a "Syllabus of Errors" which once again condemned under sixty-eight heads all principles of rationalistic philosophy destructive of belief in the after-life and in supernatural values.

Not content with that, Pius also came to grips with Modernism theoretically and practically in the combative Encyclical *Pascendi*. A decree entitled *Lamentabile* was issued by the Holy Office with the Pope's approval, wherein instructions were given for a strict supervision to be kept over the whole clergy, and orders were given for the exclusion from all educational establishments for the training of priests of any student or teacher suspected of sympathy with the new doctrines. A special *Consilium vigilantiæ* was entrusted with the duty of carrying out investigations in every diocese for the slightest trace of the modernist spirit, and of stepping in at once even against "novelties of words." Seminarists were forbidden to read newspapers and periodicals; professors had to submit their lectures to the bishops for approval, and a strict watch was to be kept over the method of teaching. Finally Pius prescribed a special "Anti-Modernist oath" to be taken by all professors and candidates for the priesthood, confessors, preachers and higher Church dignitaries, whereby they bound themselves not to participate in any movement of secular thought that ran counter to the teachings of the Church.

Indicative of his unworldly and austere spirit was the

Motu Proprio *Inter sollicitudines*, which Pius X issued immediately after his accession, and which dealt with the reform of Church music. To the ear of this zealous Pope the Masses and singing that use and custom had established in the cathedrals of Italy were too profane in character, and as in a former age the Council of Trent had conceived it a duty to bring back Church music to a purer form, now Pope Pius ordered the re-adoption of the Gregorian chant in the services of the Church. Henceforward all compositions were to be carefully examined to see that no echo of worldly operas and melodies was contained in them, and that their external form did not recall songs taken from profane sources. By such methods of censorship he hoped to prevent any taint of worldliness from creeping into the liturgy, and the soul from being distracted by sentiments of a profane character during the celebration of the mysteries.

Thus the attitude of the Church in the period immediately following the pontificate of Leo certainly deviated very materially from the policy of reconciliation that Leo had pursued. In spite of this, Pius X preserved, wherever this was possible, the spiritual inheritance of his predecessor, and passed it on to the future.

Like Leo XIII, he saw in Thomism the method of thought upon which Catholic philosophy must continue to build. Accordingly in the year 1907 he exhorted the bishops to cling firmly to scholasticism, and charged the General of the Dominicans to see that the Order placed under him should meet the "arrogant criticism of the moderns" everywhere with the Thomistic doctrine which forms a firm bulwark in the midst of errors.

As guiding principles for the judgment of social questions Pius issued a collection of sentences taken word for word from the pronouncements of Leo XIII and especially from the Encyclical *Rerum novarum*. He clearly gave it to be understood that he had nothing to add to the teachings of his predecessor on these points, and that these teachings had his whole-hearted approval.

Thus in our days Pope Pius XI is able to affirm that the Church has not suffered the "precious treasure" of Leonine doctrine "to remain unprofitably stored away," but has on the contrary dispensed it far and wide. Unceasingly Leo's successors have proclaimed and applied his teachings in word and writing, and under the guidance of the Church "many learned priests and laymen have earnestly devoted themselves to the problem of elaborating social and economic science in accordance with the conditions of our age, for the chief purpose of adapting to modern needs the unchanging and unchangeable doctrine of the Church."

*

* *

The last three weeks before the death of Pius X were filled with those disorders which attended the beginning of the World War. The reports that reached the sick chamber of the Vatican where the Pope was fighting a severe attack of pneumonia, told of armies on the march in Belgium, in the Vosges, in Poland and in Serbia, of trench-mortars, machine-guns, aircraft and torpedoes, of burning cities, shell-riddled villages, fleeing populations.

And in the hours when Benedict XV, the chosen successor of Pius X, received the homage of the Cardinals for the first time and was carried upon the *sedia gestatoria* to the coronation Mass in St. Peter's, shells were falling on Rheims Cathedral, Germans and French were battling for positions on the Aisne, the French government was fleeing from a Paris threatened by enemy guns.

For more than a century the secular philosophies of

liberalism and materialism, of technical progress and capitalist industry had accustomed men to regard themselves as masters of the earth, and now these world forces, independent of supernatural means, which were to bring about the "greatest good of the greatest number" upon earth, had been perverted into the instruments of a horrible mass slaughter. The "free economics" of liberal doctrine had been turned into a wild destruction of worldly goods; technical science, the pride of independent humanity, had been transformed into a gigantic machinery of death.

This war more than any previous one in the history of the world represented a purely material conflict between material forces and numbers. It was fought and decided with the means of technical science, and victory went to the party which had the superiority of numbers on its side, whose factories could turn out tanks, aircraft, howitzers, shells, uniforms and shoes more quickly than its opponents.

Despite his dislike of all diplomacy, Pius X was forced to recognize, in the later years of his pontificate, that the Pope has of necessity to become a politician. With Benedict XV, that accomplished ecclesiastical diplomat of the school of Leo and Rampolla, the Church returned externally at least and in accordance with the exigencies of the war situation to the paths of Leonine diplomacy. Indeed the reign of Pope Benedict has in actual fact passed into history as the "Pontificate of Concordats."

While the war was still raging, Holland decided to establish a permanent legation at the Vatican and, in stating the reason for this step, the Dutch Prime Minister, Van der Linden, declared that there "does not exist a more important political centre" than the Vatican. The view of the Dutch statesman soon proved to have been well justified. In the period immediately following the war, the Vatican achieved an international position similar to that which it had enjoyed in the time of Leo. One after another, the newly formed States, such as Poland and Jugoslavia, Finland and Czechoslovakia, took pains to establish good relations with the Vatican and even far-off Japan sent a representative to the papal court.

Even France felt impelled in the year 1921 to resume broken relations and Benedict XV, in the spirit of Pope Leo, showed himself ready to recognize accomplished facts and to suspend his opposition to French laws concerning ecclesiastical matters. On the same day that the one-time Premier Combes, who when in power had pushed matters to extremes in the anti-clerical campaign, died in obscure retirement, the newly-appointed ambassador of France to the Vatican set out on his journey for Rome.

Moreover the renewed value set upon the good-will of the Vatican also effected a change of view among Italian statesmen. Upon the death of Benedict at the beginning of the year 1922, these views found public expression in various demonstrations of sympathy. The news of the Pontiff's demise was officially recognized by the Italian Prime Minister; the Minister of Education arranged for the closing of all state schools as a mark of national mourning, and the Minister of Marine ordered the battle fleet to fly its flags at half-mast.

Although the traditions of Leo's diplomacy were revived by Pope Benedict, the pupil of Cardinal Rampolla, they could not reintegrate a world sunk into the materialism of arms or restore that system of a divinely-ordered harmony dreamed of and striven for by Leo. It is true that in 1915 the Dutch Premier had expressed the opinion that the Papacy belonged to the great Powers, and that the Pope's influence could be "of great importance in giving peace to sick humanity as soon as possible." But the course of events did not justify his optimism. Benedict exerted himself in vain to bring warring humanity to a proper frame of mind so that it might regard the principles of Christianity. Unheard were his warnings to turn away from the material madness of destruction, and to bear in mind that respect for honour and justice, and that alone, not the triumph of earthly violence, can ensure the peace of the world; that "nations do not die," that on the contrary, though they be "humbled and oppressed, they chafe under the yoke imposed upon them, preparing a renewal of the combat, and passing down from generation to generation a mournful heritage of hatred and revenge."

In the din and uproar evoked by the machinery of death, the world remained deaf to the call of the Pope. Men's brains, wholly in bondage to their "interests" and "war aims," were too dulled to comprehend; their eyes read only the words of the papal plea without perceiving the meaning and import of the message. Thus "the sons engaged in strife disregard the prayers and tears of their father," and Benedict XV was forced to lament the "failure of all his efforts . . . although We have left unused not a single occasion which promised to hasten a settlement of the disputes, yet the cruel war continues to rage on sea and on land."

The peace finally concluded in the year 1918 was by no means guided by Christian and supernatural principles. It was based solely on material considerations of an "independent" political and economic order. It simply represented the result of a struggle in which a stronger war machine had worn down a weaker one.

*

* *

From the war, like a vision of the Apocalypse, rose the greatest and most powerful enemy with which Christianity has been faced since its beginnings—the Antichrist, the "Beast without a name," Bolshevism.

This enemy first made its appearance among the Russian people, whose Orthodox Faith, separated from Catholicism for a thousand years, had led its own independent existence, so that the violent attack upon religion seemed at first only to affect the Byzantine Church. But Bolshevism signifies something more than the closing of churches and monasteries, and the expulsion and murder of Russian clergy. Its danger lies not in that antagonism to religion which Christianity of all denominations has experienced numerous times in the course of the last two thousand years; rather this danger comes from the new gospel, from the "glad tidings of Antichrist," which were now announced to the world by Bolshevism from the new order which held out to war-afflicted humanity the promise of world reorganisation and material well-being.

In Bolshevism the absolutely material religion of enlightened rationalism finds its unqualified realization. The men of the Marxian school who are engaged in building up a new political and social system and a new order of life in Russia, are working with inflexible consistency to place mankind in absolute dependence upon itself and upon earthly forces and to root out every memory of the old deeply-implanted notions of a God, a soul, an after-life or supernatural aim.

What Karl Marx once propounded in theory and demanded for the future, is becoming reality in the new Russia. The vast empire with a population of a hundred and fifty millions has been transformed into a single, thoroughly rationalised machine for production; man, to whom religion has ascribed an immortal

[159]

individual soul, becomes an exchangeable unit, a mass-particle, and belief in the existence of any values above the material is being driven from its last, remote corner and the thought and life of the Russian people.

This new empire of a mechanized proletariat is to be founded in Russia, but is then to redeem the whole world with a triumphant onrush in the name of materialism and collectivism. The Asiatic fanaticism which upheld this "Gospel of the Antichrist" on Russian soil soon carried the message to the West, to the Far East, and even across the seas. At the time of Benedict XV's death, the new doctrine had already ravaged Hungary, crossed the Alps and was threatening Catholicism in Italy itself.

Soon Mexico too was in its power and there was fanned into flame an anti-religious campaign, described by Cardinal Gasparri, the papal Secretary of State, as going far beyond any persecution of adherents of the Christian religion in the times of Nero, Caligula or Domitian. In a once completely Catholic Mexico men are now in power who, imbued with the Bolshevik spirit, aim at wiping out every vestige of religion, so that the reign of the "earthly glory of man" may begin. A decree has been issued by the Mexican Government whereby instruction in the whole Republic is to be "free from religion of any kind," and the use of the word "God" in any school is declared a punishable offence.

Moreover, in present-day Europe many non-Socialist countries are exposed to the strongest ideological and political influence from fundamental Marxism, and it seems as if even those parts of the world which stand opposed to the political régime of Bolshevism, may yet succumb in spirit to the ideas of the new economic and social order which proceed therefrom.

"The last Pope is dead!" triumphantly exclaimed a Bolshevik writer on the death of Benedict XV in 1922. Ten years later Pius XI, Benedict's successor, raised his voice and, with the authority of the appointed vicar of Christ, claimed the right to denounce Bolshevism before the whole world.

"We lay down the principle," declared the new Pope, "that in virtue of Our Apostolic office it is Our right and Our duty to deal authoritatively with social and economic problems"; and he therefore proposed "after arraigning modern economics and examining the nature of Socialism, to expose the root of the present disorder." Indeed the Pope has the weighty office, entrusted to him by God, "of propagating, interpreting, and urging, in season and out of season, the entire moral law," and this brings both social and economic questions within his "supreme jurisdiction, in so far as they refer to moral issues."

The fortieth anniversary of the day upon which Leo had issued his Encyclical *Rerum novarum* was the occasion taken by Pius XI to issue his Encyclical *Quadragesimo anno* in which he restated the social doctrine of Leo in opposition to the materialistic programme of Socialism.

The "scientific socialism" which in the days of *Rerum novarum* had been but the doctrine of a party opposition, had grown during forty years into a political power of the first importance; the cleavage of the world into two mutually hostile classes had resulted in frightful civil wars and unprecedented social upheavals and had even produced a gigantic state governed by a system of proletarian class dictatorship. But for the Church the conception which Leo had once opposed to Socialism still provides the "unerring rules for the right solution of the Social question." Hence the Encyclical *Quadragesimo anno* characterizes Leo's ideas as "admirable teaching" which in the crucial test of time has proved itself to be the surest basis for all Christian social effort; the publication of *Rerum novarum* was an event which now after forty years "the whole Catholic world gratefully recalls and prepares to celebrate with befitting solemnity."

Thus the ideas set forth in *Quadragesimo anno* are in their essential features but a recapitulation of the social doctrine of Leo, which is merely given "a more precise application and amplification" with regard to "new needs and changed conditions" that had made their appearance during the forty years between the two Encyclicals. Pius XI constantly emphasizes his conviction that Pope Leo's concept of a divinely-ordered society is not only a "beautiful and imaginary picture of human society. We should rather say that Our illustrious Predecessor drew from the Gospel, as from a living and life-giving source, doctrines capable, if not of settling at once, at least of considerably mitigating, the fatal internal strife which rends the human family."

*

* *

Pius, like Leo, recognizes the absolute necessity of a fundamental reform of social conditions. He categorically asserts that liberal and capitalist economics have shown their utter impotence to solve the social problems of the age, and sharply condemns that "irresponsible wealthy class" who "in the excess of their good fortune, deem it a just state of things that they should receive everything and the labourer nothing."

On the other hand Socialism is by no means qualified to replace liberalism; in his time Leo had realized that the remedy offered by the Socialists was "more disastrous than the evil it designed to cure." Indeed for Socialism as for liberalism man is merely an economic unit dependent on the "laws" derived from the nature of earthly goods, and society for the Socialists is nothing more than a utilitarian association for temporal ends. In that all supernatural values are "subordinated and even sacrificed to the exigencies of economic production," Socialism reverses the true gradation of ends of the Divine order, and violates the free nature of man endowed with the dignity of personality, in favour of material methods which really belong only to a subordinate grade of ends.

"The loss of human dignity, which results from these socialist methods of production is in the Marxist view easily compensated for by the abundance of goods produced in common and accruing to the individual." With the result, however, continues Pius, wholly in the spirit of Leo, that the proper meaning of life, the "sublime end both of individuals and of society" is completely ignored and the essential truth denied whereby "man, endowed with a social nature, is placed here on earth in order that he may spend his life in society, and under an authority ordained by God; that he may develop and evolve to the full all his faculties to the praise and glory of his Creator; and that, by fulfilling faithfully the duties of his station, he may attain to temporal and eternal happiness."

While it is true that "all those versed in social matters demand a rationalization of economic life which will introduce sound and true order," yet this order "will necessarily be quite faulty and imperfect," unless all man's economic activities unite "to imitate, and as far as is humanly possible, attain the marvellous unity of the Divine plan"—that "perfect order" which the Church has always preached and right reason demands, which "places God as the first and supreme end of all created activity, and regards all created goods as mere instruments under God, to be used only insofar as they help towards the attainment of our supreme end."

As every activity finds its true meaning only in metaphysical ethical values, it is quite false to assert that the "two orders of economic science and moral discipline are so distinct and alien that the former in no way depends on the latter."

True, economics has its own laws; these however are valid only for the world of material things, but not for man who in everything that concerns his conduct is subject first and foremost to the moral law. It is this alone which commands him to "strive directly in his specific actions for those ends which nature, or rather the author of nature has established for them."

Accordingly practical remunerative occupations, as Leo had already taught, are ennobled and sanctified through being pursued in harmony with the divine plan. The acquisition of earthly goods, again, is justified provided always that he who acquires them "respects the laws of God and the rights of his neighbour, and uses his property in accord with faith and right reason." If the moral law be faithfully obeyed, the result will be that "particular economic aims, whether of society as a body or of individuals, will be intimately linked with the universal teleological order, and as a consequence we shall be led by progressive stages to the final end of all, God Himself, our highest and lasting good."

Accordingly the striving of Socialism for a just distribution of temporal goods rests according to Pius XI on a complete deception, since a mechanical, purely material "commutative justice" that takes count only of earthly relations can never bring about that interior "union of hearts and minds," which forms an indispensable condition for lasting social peace: "Then only will it be possible to unite all in harmonious striving for the common good, when all sections of society have the intimate conviction that they are members of a single family and children of the same Heavenly Father, and further, that they are 'one body in Christ, and everyone members one of another.'"

Whereas the mechanical conception of Socialism reaches out towards the ideal of a homogeneous, undifferentiated mass and of a "classless society," Pius XI renews with special emphasis the demand already expressed by Leo for a reorganization of society on a functional or vocational basis. In order to abolish conflict between classes with divergent interests, "well-ordered members of the social body" should be formed, or in other words, "vocational groups binding men together not according to the position they occupy in the labour-market, but according to the diverse functions which they exercise in society."

If all the members of such a social organism always keep the common good as their predominant aim, the whole system of vocational groups, despite manifold differences as regards rights and duties, will work organically together in the spirit of a general solidarity: indeed, order as St. Thomas well defines, is "unity arising from the apt arrangement of a plurality of objects."

In such a society every effort will be made to the end that a "just share only of the fruits of production be permitted to accumulate in the hands of the wealthy, and that an ample sufficiency be supplied to the working-men." What is to be achieved thereby is the overcoming of class-conflicts not by the abolition of property and by universal proletarianism, such as Bolshevism aims at, but by the "de-proletarianisation of the proletariate."

Though the Church puts forward this programme as a solution of the social problem, nevertheless it is far from her intention, insists Pius XI, to interfere in technical matters, "for which she has neither the equipment nor the mission"; but she will not and cannot relinquish her God-given task of interposing her authority where it is a question of "man's eternal happiness," of the ordination of secondary causes to the first and highest Cause, that is to say, in everything that has a bearing on the moral law.

"If we examine matters diligently and thoroughly," declares the Encyclical *Quadragesimo anno* in its final summing up, "we shall perceive clearly that the longed-for social reconstruction must be preceded by a profound renewal of the Christian spirit, from which multitudes engaged in industry in every country have unhappily departed. Otherwise, all our endeavours will be futile, and our social edifice will be built, not upon a rock, but upon shifting sand.

"'And if society is to be healed now—We use the words of Our Predecessors—in no way can it be healed save by a return to Christian life and Christian institutions.' For Christianity alone can apply an efficacious remedy for the excessive solicitude for transitory things, which is the origin of all vices. When men are fascinated by, and completely absorbed in, the things of the world, it alone can draw away their attention and raise it to heaven. And who will deny that this remedy is now urgently needed by society?"

4

The publication of Leo's Encyclical, *Æterni Patris*, wherein he proclaimed that the reconciliation of faith with reason, of the Church with the world, must be sought and attained on the lines of the doctrine of entelechy and Thomistic principles of order, had evoked a great deal of hostile criticism. The attempt to meet modern thought with the formulae of scholasticism, to rebuild the prosaic, complicated, mechanized structure of modern life on the basis of ethical concepts was characterized as a hopeless undertaking foredoomed to failure. Indeed Leo's endeavour could but seem reactionary and reprehensible, since it obviously aimed at arresting the development of humanity by the rehabilitation of a mediæval philosophy, and in this way "to put back the clock."

Even in many Catholic circles misgivings were aroused concerning the Thomist revival initiated by Leo and doubts were openly expressed as to whether the arduous struggle in which Faith was engaged against the thought of modern times, could really be fought to a successful issue with the help of the scholastic system. Well-meaning critics saw in the Encyclical *Æterni Patris* a "regrettable anachronism damaging to the Church" and suggested that the Pope would do far better to "speak to his age in a language it could understand," instead of repeating arguments with which mediæval theologians, proceeding from quite different hypotheses, had championed views that had long since become obsolete.

Nevertheless throughout all the spiritual changes that have followed Leo's pontificate, the Church has continued unshaken to regard Thomism as the basis of the Catholic philosophy of life and of Catholic economic and social policy. In an Encyclical published on the occasion of the sixth centenary of the canonization of St. Thomas, Pius XI stated categorically that the *princeps scholasticorum* was the guide to be followed in all higher philosophical studies, as it was preeminent both in theology and philosophy and gave "infallible rules and precepts of life" not only for individuals but also for society. "If these precepts were religiously and inviolably observed in private life and public affairs, and in the duties of mutual obligation between nations, nothing else would be required to secure mankind that 'peace of Christ in the Kingdom of Christ' which the world so ardently longs for."

The philosophical views of believers in progress quarrel with these theses no less violently today than in the time of Leo's Encyclical. Certainly in comparison with the unreasoning, ascetic and mystical Christianity of pre-Thomistic times and in comparison with the attitude of such Popes as Gregory IX and Gregory XVI, or even Pius IX, the Thomistic line of approach towards a settlement with rationalistic forces and with the realities of modern life as pursued by Leo XIII and now by Pius XI seems to present a more modern, more progressive, attitude. But does not it too remain irrevocably bound up in the spirit of reaction, in that it endeavours to reach the desired understanding and reconciliation with modern times by methods which have long been left behind and discarded in the course of spiritual and material developments?

Do not Leo and Pius both ignore the spiritual and material distance which separates the twentieth from the thirteenth century, and is it not just in this disregard of evolution that lies the obscurantism with which modern "enlightened" man has always reproached the Church?

*

* *

There seems to exist a misunderstanding in the very fact that the Church today is still trying by means of

Thomism to bring faith and reason into accord, whereas modern rationalism has hardly anything in common with the kind of reason which Aquinas had in mind. Aristotle had been the thinker who represented rational philosophy for Thomas; but the rationalist thought of our time has its origin in revolt against Aristotelian syllogisms and deductions. Natural sciences have furnished the foundations of the modern world-concept; in the days of Thomas, however, these sciences were still nothing more than the secret knowledge of a select few. So little were they common property at that time, that Thomas, in his otherwise comprehensive *Summa* virtually ignored them. Roger Bacon, on the other hand, the only contemporary of Aquinas' upon whom a cognitive understanding of the most important natural sciences had dawned, was imprisoned for these very views.

Though reason had passed through epochal transformations as a result of its contacts with Enlightenment, empiricism, subjectivism and critical philosophy, all of which had afforded multiform new sciences and points of view, the profane world of purely mundane interests had passed through changes equally impressive since the days when Thomas believed he had embedded them in the soil of the higher realm of the Transcendental. The increasing "worldliness" of life, which Aquinas confronted in that epoch of early capitalism, consisted merely in the fact that men who thitherto had lived for the next world in a spirit of prayer and discipline, now learned to know the charms of material pleasures, began to hanker after silks and spices, and took no heed of the law against taking interest on money.

Thomas had grasped the autonomous laws which prevailed in this sphere of budding trade and travel, where people strove to have their fill of material, terrestrial things; and he knew how to subordinate these laws under an assumed higher world of "first causes." Yet just as the natural sciences became the foundation of a wholly new philosophy, so also did the material manifestation of these sciences — the machine — create a radically different kind of human life. It effected so great an upheaval of the whole nature of humanity that the very face of the earth was altered. And therefore the Church of the nineteenth and twentieth centuries had to wrestle with a world which had become totally different from the globe of St. Thomas' time. Even during the short span of years between Leo XIII and Pius XI — the four decades which separate *Rerum novarum* from *Quadragesimo anno* — such changes took place that it all seems fantastic in retrospect.

Pius XI has himself admitted that since the time of Leo the "entire economic scene has greatly changed." The world-wide diffusion of capitalist industry has pervaded even the social and economic sphere of those who live outside the capitalist sphere, affecting them by its advantages, inconveniences and vices. The fact that not only is wealth accumulated, but that "immense power and despotic economic domination is concentrated in the hands of a few, and that those few are frequently not the owners, but only the trustees and directors of invested funds," has created conditions such as could hardly have been foreseen in the lifetime of Leo.

Thus, although a spiritual and material development of more than six hundred years has moved away from Thomistic doctrine — and that moreover a period in which the greatest and most transforming events in the history of mankind (the discovery of the natural sciences and the rise of the machine) had taken place —

yet Leo XIII made the Thomistic concept of the world the basis of Catholic philosophy and sociology. The Church of Pius XI in our day proclaims anew her resolve, regardless of progress and change — no matter how fundamental — in the ideas and social formations of the world, to remain true to that principle of Thomism and Leo. Again she endeavours, by means of the Thomistic doctrine of the two orders, to subordinate profane thought and the world of material happenings to a higher transcendental order.

*

* *

And yet it is exceedingly difficult to dismiss the teachings of the Church as the pious illusions of a sect, and to pretend that today as in the times of Comte, Catholicism, succumbing to spiritual inertia, remains wrapped in an obsolete world of mediæval ideas and concepts, and that it represents a backward stage of cultural development.

Such a view is contradicted not least by the incontestable fact that the Church herself had no small share in the intellectual and cultural development of the West, and that countless believers, and not a few priests, are to be found among the great leaders of scientific research. And today do not millions of persons of high standing in intellectual, professional and cultural life adhere with profound conviction to Catholic teaching? Do not many minds, whose scientific attitude is beyond all doubt, believe in the possibility and justification of that Thomistic system of classification?

The movement which we call the Enlightenment had expressed the need for intellectual development which in order to arrive at new cognitions had to break the bans of tradition. Thus, for men of the age of the Enlightenment to combat the theological conception of the

[171]

world by all possible means and to dis
actionary and outmoded, had seemed a
necessity.   At that time the depreciatio
seem justified from the position of the
historical truth must again step into its
jective survey at once raises the quest
relationship between Catholicism and
philosophy, between belief in a king
dental truths and the conviction of the
bility of the world to natural causations
expressed   by   the   formulas   "ret
"progress."

A knowledge of the history of West
lishes the fact that by no means in
arguments of those thinkers who sou
knowledge to rationally demonstrable
themselves as new and superior ne
every transcendental philosophy of
retire.   On the contrary, a survey of
opment shows that a purely ration
explanation of every happening ex
entelechist, and that as against
the teachings of a Plato and an Ari
the character of a step forward.

It was not in ignorance of the po
ing the world mechanistically and
Aristotle, for example, had constru
in conscious opposition to views
familiar to him.   Critical comment
sors contained all arguments for an
and independent individualism.   I
polemic against the empiricists of t
ment when Aristotle charges Demo
the view that his mechanistic the
satisfactory explanation of final

yet Leo XIII made the Thomistic concept of the world the basis of Catholic philosophy and sociology. The Church of Pius XI in our day proclaims anew her resolve, regardless of progress and change—no matter how fundamental—in the ideas and social formations of the world, to remain true to that principle of Thomism and Leo. Again she endeavours, by means of the Thomistic doctrine of the two orders, to subordinate profane thought and the world of material happenings to a higher transcendental order.

*

* *

And yet it is exceedingly difficult to dismiss the teachings of the Church as the pious illusions of a sect, and to pretend that today as in the times of Comte, Catholicism, succumbing to spiritual inertia, remains wrapped in an obsolete world of mediæval ideas and concepts, and that it represents a backward stage of cultural development.

Such a view is contradicted not least by the incontestable fact that the Church herself had no small share in the intellectual and cultural development of the West, and that countless believers, and not a few priests, are to be found among the great leaders of scientific research. And today do not millions of persons of high standing in intellectual, professional and cultural life adhere with profound conviction to Catholic teaching? Do not many minds, whose scientific attitude is beyond all doubt, believe in the possibility and justification of that Thomistic system of classification?

The movement which we call the Enlightenment had expressed the need for intellectual development which in order to arrive at new cognitions had to break the bans of tradition. Thus, for men of the age of the Enlightenment to combat the theological conception of the

[171]

world by all possible means and to disparage it as reactionary and outmoded, had seemed a direct biological necessity. At that time the depreciation of faith might seem justified from the position of the battle; but now historical truth must again step into its own. An objective survey at once raises the question whether the relationship between Catholicism and a purely secular philosophy, between belief in a kingdom of transcendental truths and the conviction of the absolute reducibility of the world to natural causations, can be properly expressed by the formulas "retrogression" and "progress."

A knowledge of the history of Western culture establishes the fact that by no means in every case do the arguments of those thinkers who sought to reduce all knowledge to rationally demonstrable elements, present themselves as new and superior news, before which every transcendental philosophy of the world has to retire. On the contrary, a survey of intellectual development shows that a purely rational and materialistic explanation of every happening existed prior to the entelechist, and that as against those philosophies the teachings of a Plato and an Aristotle had precisely the character of a step forward.

It was not in ignorance of the possibility of conceiving the world mechanistically and unteleologically that Aristotle, for example, had constructed his system, but in conscious opposition to views that were perfectly familiar to him. Critical commentaries on his predecessors contained all arguments for and against rationalism and independent individualism. Indeed it sounds like a polemic against the empiricists of the age of Enlightenment when Aristotle charges Democritus of Abdera with the view that his mechanistic theory leads to no more satisfactory explanation of final causes than the sentence: "It is so or always happens so." In Protagoras also, Aristotle combats a philosopher who, with the statement that man with his cognitive thinking was "the measure of all things" and that there existed no absolute but only a relative truth, had outlined in advance the whole development of philosophic doubt up to Descartes and Kant.

Similarly St. Thomas, in the thousands of "objections," which, in accordance with the scholastic method, he brings against his own theses, did not overlook any of the objections noted by Aristotle against the entelechist and teleological conception of the universe; and he likewise knew already and submitted to the closest consideration the majority of the theories that have been opposed to his system in later times. Thus in St. Thomas' commentaries on Aristotle we find an examination of the teleological principle in nature which anticipates the whole basic idea of Darwinism — the assumption of a "natural selection" in the struggle for existence — though he rejects this hypothesis in the end, and sets against it the theological view.

*

* *

Not merely in the past — no, quite decidedly in our own living present — have intellectual developments made it seem more and more questionable whether the absolute superiority of the "teleophobic" over the teleological philosophy can be assumed. For much water has flowed under the bridge since the Enlightenment, which repudiated the transcendental in every form, was followed by a scientific trend which again favored many elements of the doctrine of entelechy.

If Hans Driesch has shown that a sea urchin when cut into four parts matures of itself into four complete, only correspondingly smaller, sea urchins; that consequently each of the mechanically divided quarters is able to evolve out of itself the whole, perfect form, then it is obvious that this constancy of form can only be explained on the hypothesis of a teleological striving, inherent in the living creature and not causally comprehensible.

This one example taken from biology suffices to prove that it is not so "barren and fruitless" to look for "final causes" in nature as Bacon supposed. "A plant becomes really comprehensible to us only when we look upon it as the working out of a unitarian entelechy," writes Richard Mueller-Frienfels. "It is true that heat, light, the presence of water and nitrogen and carbonic acid gas, etc., are prerequisites to the manifestation of the entelechy. We can likewise coordinate the separate heat, light and chemical processes with other, similar processes observed while studying other beings, and then state them in the form of general laws. But the fact that all these different 'laws' operate together in this one case, and the fact that there is a purposive sequence of separate processes, cannot be accounted for by referring to the laws themselves. The key can only be the entelechial activity of the plant itself, which utilizes these outer forces to achieve its purpose. The presence of law, in so far as it is mechanico-rational, applies only in that there is a relative amount of uniformity. It does not help us to account for the individuation of the real. Accordingly we can account for the world of individual entities only by conceiving of them as striving totalities and by interpreting what goes on in them, by analogy with our own nature, as an integration of lower energies into higher energies."

Belief in a transcendental end of all being has constantly made its appearance from ancient times to the present day. Thus it must be recognized that the opposition between the teleological and mechanistic conceptions of the universe, between the view that the world is shaped toward a metaphysical and perfect realm and that it is restricted to the certainties of observation or of critical thought, cannot be explained simply as the conflict between two points of view, one backward, the other advanced.

The Thomist system in particular proves itself as the logical and formally complete expression of a philosophy which stands in eternal opposition to the search for knowledge based on man's unaided reason. It seems to be constitutionally implanted in thought itself, and therefore neither represents the product of a definite epoch of time nor can it be overcome in the process of evolution. Both these fundamental attitudes of the mind, underlying each of which is an elemental spiritual urge, have conflicted with one another from the beginning and have successively supplanted each other in their turn. Each strives for a completion of its concept of the universe — one as a cosmos in which everything, including the apparently supernatural, can be reduced to known laws explained by physical principles and capable of positive proof, the other as an ordination of all existing things to a metaphysical end which gives them their whole meaning.

Protagoras, Democritus, Descartes, Bacon, Galileo, Kant and Darwin were all driven to their philosophical and scientific opinions by an urge for knowledge which gave them no rest in their search for an indestructible basis of rational cognition. On the other hand Plato and Aristotle, Thomas and Leo, allowed themselves to be guided in their philosophical conceptions by the inner certitude that beyond the world of perception and understanding, a final higher end is to be sought and found, and that without this the whole of creation is meaningless.

Viewed in this light, Leo's XIII's great attempt to order the thought and activity of modern mankind in conformity with a supernatural conception can no longer be regarded as an attempt "to put back the clock." But has not the course of events since Leo's *Rerum novarum* demonstrated the impossibility of any such subordination of earthly life to transcendental principles? Does the world of our day seem ready to submit piously and humbly to the doctrines of the Encyclical *Quadragesimo anno*, in which the present Pope proclaims anew the doctrines of Leo? Does not the whole range of human activity unceasingly disavow belief in the divinely ordered universe which was dreamed of by St. Thomas and his papal disciples?

Perhaps. But it has always been the way of the world to disavow everything the spirit has conceived. It has also confounded the dreams of a State founded upon reason, and the striving for a rationalistic, materialistic world order. Dead are Voltaire, Robespierre, Comte and the other great "Masters of the Lodge," who in their lay "encyclicals" proclaimed the reconstruction of the world according to the principles of progress, and their visions went with them to the grave. Material order regulated by reason alone has no more achieved stable reality than the supernatural order of the Church.

Nevertheless, as the failure of the mechanistic and rational plans for world salvation does not detract from the greatness of the undertaking, the programme of the Church with its metaphysical ends ought not to be despised because of its failure to convert itself into reality. For the practical realization of an idea is always only a part of its reality, and not even the most important part. What awakens life in the spirit is of real significance for the destiny of future generations, as a challenge for ever asserting itself anew, unloosing forces, pointing the way.

5

In the time of Christ, the reason of the ancients which had ruled the world in absolute sovereignty and directed the course of human thought, determining the arrangements and social order of States, had reached the end of its reign. In the Academy at Athens where Plato and Aristotle once taught, doubt had firmly established itself. First, disputing the theories of these masters, and then, driven on by the incessant desire for truth, it had narrowed the limits of absolute knowledge, demolished one conviction after another, until finally the last scrap of rational certainty had crumbled away.

In this fateful hour of our civilization arose the Christian Faith — the belief in a truth not rationally comprehensible, in revelation, miracles, the supernatural. A significant scene in the Gospel of St. John may be taken as a turning point in the history of the human spirit. The captive Saviour says to the Roman procurator Pilate: "For this was I born, and for this came I into the world: that I should give testimony to the truth. Every one that is of the truth, heareth my voice." But Pilate, a representative of that ancient reason which was dissolving in doubt, answered the words of Jesus with a question which expresses the complete uncertainty of a system of thought which does not know what to make of its own knowledge or of any other: "What is truth?"

With this question reason gave itself up, the rationalism of the ancients came to an end. A short time afterwards the disciples of the carpenter's son from Galilee, by sacrifice of their lives, bore witness in multitudes to the supernatural truth of revelation, and from then on for more than a thousand years, generation after generation put its faith in that truth which proceeds not from human reason but from the word of God.

But neither was the certainty of faith to hold unlimited sway for all time. Reason, which had been done to death on the lips of Pilate, rose again at a time when faith was proclaiming its triumph in every land and city of the Middle Ages — and once more gaining ascendancy over the mind, captured in rapid succession the chairs of universities and penetrated even into the innermost places of devout hearts. Now for the second time the destiny of reason fulfills itself; for the second time it has gone, as in antiquity, from doubt to doubt, until in our time it again asks Pilate's question: "What is truth?"

Just therein is the especial character of rationalist thinking revealed — its independence of every fate that has its origin in outer causes. Rationalism was never conquered, either in the ancient or in our modern time, by the forces which opposed it. Neither then nor today can the might of that which is above reason triumph over, refute or silence it. No, reason has always dared to cross swords with such enemies outside itself. Armed with the most gleaming weapons of the spirit, and led by such illustrious strategists as the sceptics of antiquity, the Encyclopedists of the eighteenth century, and the great savants of recent materialism, it has withstood the shock of every attack.

Refusing to thank any other power for its inception, but proudly affirming that it has produced itself in the here-and-now, it also does not accept the death-blow from an alien hand. This last it deals out to itself, and itself determines the time and manner of its decease — so that in birth and death it may manifest its proud na-

[178]

ture, which refuses to acknowledge dependence upon any incomprehensible and divine power.

*

* *

After incomparable triumphs, after a long period of unlimited dominion over the minds of men, after the era of natural science, of the Enlightenment, of critical philosophy, of materialism and of technical science, the suicidal impulse of reason seems to have chosen our century for the end of its present reign. Accordingly we of the present day are in at the death of rationalism, and we are witnessing a process similar to the abdication of rational knowledge two thousand years ago. What took place in the Academy at Athens is now being enacted in the chairs of European and American universities, in observatories and in laboratories, and from continent to continent we hear many voices which ask again the question of Pilate.

What hitherto has passed for undisputed truth has come to nought before the searching analysis of disintegrating doubt. The empiricism on which Bacon relied, the mathematics which Descartes introduced into philosophy, the natural law which appeals to experiment for its verification — none of these forms of human rational knowledge has been able to withstand the stern, ruthless examination of reason in its fanatical quest for truth.

The men who in their laboratories carry on one experiment after another or bend over tabulated figures of astronomical and physical calculations have finally come to the conclusion that all their knowledge is in some way or another unprovable, that every answer brings up a new question, and that consequently nothing can longer justify the claim of reason to explain wholly and absolutely all things between earth and heaven. The mechanistic and rationalistic concept of the universe, which for centuries past has contended for dominion over thought with the metaphysical system of Thomism, has collapsed. Reason, which was so sure of itself, empirical inquiry with its experimental proofs, which even in the nineteenth century still deemed itself capable of refuting and unmasking the theocratic concept, has admitted its own inadequacy and cannot do enough to prove how little can actually be proved by means of its own proofs!

Philosophy has turned away from rationalism and proclaims instead the irrational powers of the will, of life, of the *élan vital*, of *violence*. Under the banner of Schopenhauer it combats the last remnant of the "enlightened" spirit, in that it recognizes the primacy of will over reason; with Nietzsche it has learned to believe once again in the instinctive forces, to recognize the "will to power" as a creative, formative element and "to give the earth a meaning."

Psychology, in place of the mechanistic theories of functions, has established belief in the subconscious. The conception of history no longer adheres to materialistic and economic causes, but rather to a "primary happening," a "creative power," and "organic becoming" of cultures and cultural cycles. Whereas a machine-like, determinist motive power was formerly considered as the basis of all phenomena, there now triumphs the belief in a biological, irrational and vital hatching and plotting of nature, and in place of the "thoroughly rationalized mechanical man" has entered the "living creature determined by biological instincts."

*

* *

Now it becomes evident that the mechanistic and materialistic world concept was only a mask, and that behind this time-conditioned form of expression, unaffected by its destruction, man's elemental will to permanence in this world still persists. This age which puts ever narrower limits to the sphere of rational knowledge and relinquishes ever larger domains to the rule of the irrational, nevertheless holds stubbornly to the conviction that the newly-recognized irrational is also "of this world." It thus obeys to the full the exhortation of Nietzsche, who cried: "Remain true to the earth, oh my brother!" However opposed this "irrationalism" may appear to be to "rationalism," this "will" to "reason," this "biologism" to "mechanism," this "living creature" to the "machine," this "subconscious" to the "conscious" — in their deepest origin and end they likewise confess to the earth, to man and to this life. For according to the new viewpoint all values lie in this world; everything is related to terrestrial being, to nature.

The thinkers who proclaim that reason is only a partial function of life, which must be subordinated and coordinated into the whole, mean by this "whole" not the Thomistic interpretation of nature and supernature, but the totality of all earthly forces of biologic and natural being. And whenever in the course of modern investigations the belief in an entelechy again emerges, this is not, as in Thomist and Aristotelian philosophy, recognized as a striving towards the Beyond, leading from the physical world to spiritual realms. On the contrary, it is conceived merely as a "form-impulse" operative in nature, which has achieved its end when the form inherent in it is realized.

It almost seems as though Duport, a deputy to the French Revolutionary Convention at the end of the eighteenth century, had with unconscious foresight predicted the destiny of human thought for a long time to come when he exclaimed: "Reason and Nature, there you have our gods!" Now, after reigning for only three generations, the goddess of Reason has fallen and the goddess Nature steps into her place, and once more thought shuts itself off from the supernatural, denies it altogether and, willing to rise no higher than this earth, accepts its human limitations.

Yes, even "truth," which all human activity has ultimately to serve, is for modern secular thought not a final and unchangeable metaphysical quantity outside man, but a "quality of the living substance," corresponding to Goethe's saying: "Only the fruitful is true." From this quality of the living substance the meaning and content of good and evil is to be determined anew.

*

* *

The abdication of rationalist thought also brought with it as a necessary consequence the collapse of the laicized State, which had been in every respect the creation of that rationalism and was intended to represent in all its institutions and aims the realization of an "enlightened" world order. The end of this laicized State came first precisely in the place where during the nineteenth century it had most defiantly established itself, where it stood out against the Vatican citadel of belief in another world; where, opposite the papal cross, it erected a statue to Giordano Bruno, the apostle of reason; where the grand exponents of anti-clericalism and the Sovereign Pontiff could, as it were, stare at each other through their windows.

That Rome of Crispi and Lemmi, which the Masonic leaders had dreamed of as the "eternal city" of free thought, now became the home of Fascism, which constructed a new State on the irrational values of myth, authority and hierarchy, and whose creator proudly announced that he was come to abolish everything that the rationalist revolution of the eighteenth century had effected. Yes, this same Rome soon witnessed the arrest of the brethren of the Masonic lodges, who now had to pay the penalty of deportation for their faith in the ideal of a vanished rationalistic age.

Ten years later the German people to whom democrats and socialists had taught a thoroughly rational conception of the State, confessed to National Socialism, and in one vast funeral pyre the whole body of rationalistic and democratic literature went up in flames.

But again, just as the changed thought of the time, in spite of its movement towards the irrational, still remains true to this earthly plane, so do the new authoritarian States that have sprung from irrational values perceive their foundations, their efficient forces and their end wholly in this world. Although these new orders acknowledge other values than those of liberalism and democracy, although they recognize irrational ties and connections and hierarchical organizations, and although all this seems to approximate to Catholic conceptions, there is yet much that separates these political movements from the teachings of the Church.

For Catholicism all hierarchy and order in the State as in society derive from a transcendental divine principle standing above created nature. Fascism and National Socialism, though they reject the socialistic ideal of classless equality in the mechanized mass, consider their hierarchy as of purely earthly origin and significance, without any reference to the divine institution and consecration of offices. The basis on which society is now to be organized rests solely on processes of natural selection symbolized in myths — on the *élan vital*, on evolution, or again on the no less nature-bound biological heritage of race. It is in conformity with these considerations that the national community is formed, that rights and duties are determined, from them that all power and authority derives its legitimacy.

Although the materialistic conception of history — which regards all religion as a superstructure based on purely economic conditions — is now stigmatized as a crime against the spirit of history, the theory which takes its place is scarcely more satisfactory since it makes man the product of his biological destiny, refusing any place to the influence of the supernatural. As earthy as its foundations are the ends which this political irrationalism sets for itself. The supreme end of all activity is not the fulfilment of a God-given mission, the greater glory of God, but rather the greater glory of the nation and its biological development to the greatest possible perfection.

*

* *

Accordingly the collapse of the "rationalist State" and the creation of new State-forms constructed on irrational values, by no means implies for the Church a cessation of that opposition which, for more than a century, has been manifested towards her by the secular powers. Again the Church in her struggle against these powers and the false ideas of the age avails herself of the principle of order defined by Leo XIII and seeks, as did Leo, to bring events in the sphere of secondary causes into proper relation with the higher sphere of the Divine.

In the age of laicism the Church strove to give reason as wide a field as possible, although it continued to subordinate its cognitions to the truth of revelation. Now she recognizes within certain limits the justification of the new, irrational world concept, in order at the same time to integrate it to a higher irrationalism which no longer finds its beginning and its end in this world. Thus, where it was once necessary to reconcile reason with what was beyond reason, now the irrationalism of beliefs rooted in myths of nation and race have to be brought into harmony with the irrationalism of belief in revealed religion.

When Fascism in particular seeks to make the national State the highest factor in the life of its citizens, the Church appeals once more to Leo XIII's Encyclical upon the duties of citizenship, in which it is laid down that the State in its sphere of secondary causes has as its end to promote the perfection of man as regards his physical and social well-being, but that this end may be pursued only in accord with the highest ends of the "moral and religious nature of man."

The Church also tries to find a place in the Thomistic hierarchy of end for the idea of race, and she certainly recognizes the importance of the stream of biological inheritance; at the same time, however, she points out that such biological descent must never be set above the spiritual descent of all men from God. Body and blood belong to the earthly sphere of secondary causes; soul and spirit, however, to the Beyond, in relation to which all the things of this world should be regarded only as serviceable means. What is inherited therefore is a "mere dress in which the spirit works out a destiny prepared by itself." Thus the Church views and values race within the natural and supernatural unity of mankind and joins subjection to the earth and spiritual origin, soul and body, to a divine order.

For the Church wills "to cover in her embrace all

[185]

terrestrial space and time, yes, even the after-life and eternity, and, despite existing differences in races, cultures, languages, and politics, to unite the nations on a Christian basis through the same spiritual descent, and to form a unity of nations in the spiritual and supernatural."

Thus in face of the aims and struggles of our day the Church takes up a position which corresponds in all essentials to the principles laid down by Leo XIII. She does not reject the new with unceremonious haste, nor does she accept it unconditionally; rather does she give it careful examination to see whether and within which sphere the programmes of the day can be recognized without conflict with her dogmatic foundations. To-day it is being proved again, that though many details of Thomistic doctrine may have lost their validity with the passing of time, yet that Leo XIII took over from Thomas and awakened to new life something that in principle may have just as much value at the present time as in the Middle Ages: the timeless principle of a higher and a lower order, which seeks truth not merely on the planes of matter and sense but in a harmony of the physical and the metaphysical whole.

BIBLIOGRAPHY

Adamow-Lambsdorff, E.: Die Diplomatie des Vatikans zur Zeit des Imperialismus. R. Hobbing, Berlin 1932.

Aster, E. v.: Die Geschichte der Philosophie. Ullstein, Berlin 1925.

Barth: Gedichte Leos XIII. 1904.

Bastgen, H.: Die römische Frage. Herder, Freiburg 1917.

Baumgartner, A.: Papst Leo XIII. Herder, Freiburg 1903.

Baunard L.: Lèo XIII et le toast d'Alger. Paris 1914.

Bavink, B.: Die Naturwissenschaft auf dem Wege zur Religion. Frankfurt 1933.

Bazin, R.: Pius X. Sands & Co., London 1928.

Becker, O.: Das französisch-russische Bündnis (Bismarck und die Einkreisung Deutschlands). Berlin 1925.

Benn, G.: Nach dem Nihilismus. G. Kiepenheuer, Berlin 1932.

Benz, R.: Geist und Reich. E. Diederichs, Jena 1933.

Bergmann, E.: Die 25 Thesen der Deutschreligion.

Bergmann, E.: Die Deutsche Nationalkirche.

Bernhart, J: Der Vatikan als Thron der Welt. P. List, Leipzig 1930.

Bie, R.: Das katholische Europa. R. Voigtländer, Leipzig 1931.

Böhtlingk, A.: Bismarck und das päpstliche Rom. Puttkammer & Mühlbrecht, Berlin 1911.

Boyer d' Agens: Die Prälatur des Papstes Leo XIII. gemäss dessen bis jetzt unveröffentl. Briefen. Manz, Regensburg 1902.

Brandes, G.: Voltaire und sein Jahrhundert. E. Reiss, Berlin.

Breitenstein, D.: Geist oder Blut? Bonifacius-Druckerei, Paderborn 1934.

Brentano, F. C.: Die vier Phasen der Philosophie und ihr augenblicklicher Stand. (Herausgegeb. v. O. Kraus), F. Meiner, Leipzig 1926.

Brosch, M.: Geschichte der europäischen Staaten. F. A. Perthes, Gotha 1880.

Brosch, M.: Geschichte des Kirchenstaates, 1880/82.

Graetz, H.: Volkstümliche Geschichte der Juden. O. Leiner, Leipzig 1914.

Granderath, Th.: Geschichte de Vatikanischen Konzils. Herder, Freiburg 1903.

Gregorovius, F.: Geschichte der Stadt Rom im Mittelalter. Stuttgart 1926.

Grisar, H.: History of Rome and the Popes in the Middle Ages. Paul, Trench, Trübner & Co., London 1911/12.

Gröber, C.: Nationalkirche? Herder, Freiburg 1934.

Grupp, G.: Kulturgeschichte des Mittelalters. F. Schöningh, Paderborn 1924.

Güdemann, M.: Jüdische Kulturgeschichte im Mittelalter. Berlin 1922.

Gundlach, H.: Die sozialen Rundschreiben Leos XIII. und Pius XI. F. Schöningh, Paderborn 1931.

Haessle, J.: Das Arbeitsethos der Kirche. Herder, Freiburg 1923.

Haller, J.: Das Papsttum. Idee und Wirklichkeit. J. G. Cotta, Stuttgart-Berlin 1934.

Hampe, K.: Belgiens Vergangenheit und Gegenwart. B. G. Teubner, Leipzig-Berlin 1915.

Harnack, A.: Das Testament Leos XIII. (In: Preussische Jahrbücher, Bd. 77). H. Walther, Berlin 1894.

Hartmann, C.: Christentum und Deutschreligion. Bonifacius-Druckerei, Paderborn 1934.

Hartmann, O.: Der Kampf um den Menschen in Natur, Mythos, Geschichte. R. Oldenbourg, München 1934.

Heiler, F.: Der Katholizismus, seine Idee und seine Erscheinung. E. Reinhardt, München 1934.

Hellwald, F. v.: Culturgeschichte in ihrer natürlichen Entwicklung bis zur Gegenwart. Lampart, Augsburg 1877.

Hessen, J.: Die Weltanschauung des Thomas von Aquin. Strecker & Schröder, Stuttgart 1926.

Hettinger: Die kirchliche Vollgewalt des Apostolischen Stuhles. Freiburg 1873.

Hoensbroech, Graf v.: Das Papsttum in seiner sozial-kulturellen Wirksamkeit. Breitkopf & Härtel, Leipzig 1900.

Honegger, J.: Grundsteine einer Allgemeinen Culturgeschichte der neuesten Zeit. J. J. Weber, Leipzig 1874.

Jansen, B.: Descartes, der Vater der heutigen Philosophie.

Eine unzeitgemässe Betrachtung. (Stimmen der Zeit, Heft 11, August 1927). Herder, Freiburg.

Jansen, B.: Zur neuesten Geschichte der alten Philosophie. (Stimmen der Zeit, 6. Heft, März 1926). Herder, Freiburg.

Jansen, B.: Wege der Weltweisheit. Herder, Freiburg 1924.

Jansen, B.: Der Kampf um Augustinus im 13. Jahrhundert. (Stimmen der Zeit, 8. Heft, Mai 1926). Herder, Freiburg.

Jansen, B.: Moderne Denker und Neuscholastik. (Stimmen der Zeit, Heft 3, Dezemb. 1926). Herder, Freiburg.

Jansen, B.: Die Wesensform des katholischen Lebens. (Stimmen der Zeit, Heft 1, Okt. 1926). Herder, Freiburg.

Judet, E.: Le Vatican et la paix de Léon XIII à Pie XI. Paris 1927.

Karpeles, G.: Geschichte der Jüdischen Literatur. R. Oppenheim, Berlin 1886.

Katholische Arbeitervereine Westdeutschlands: Die Rundschreiben Leos XIII. und Pius XI. Tat-Verlag, Köln 1932.

Kayserling: Geschichte der Juden in Spanien und Portugal. Springer, Berlin 1861.

Keller, L.: Die geistigen Grundlagen der Freimaurerei und das öffentl. Leben. E. Diederichs, Jena 1911.

Kissling, J.: Geschichte des Kulturkampfes im Deutschen Reich. Freiburg 1916.

Klagges, D.: Idee und System. Vorträge an der Deutschen Hochschule für Politik über Grundfragen nationalsozialistischer Weltanschauung. Armanen-Verlag, Leipzig 1934.

Kliem, K.: Der Papst im Völkerrecht. K. Abele, München 1932.

Knaurs Weltgeschichte: Von der Urzeit bis zur Gegenwart. (Herausgegeb. v. K. A. v. Müller u. P. R. Rohden). Th. Knaur, Berlin 1935.

Koch, A.: Völkerchaos und Völkerkirche. (Stimmen der Zeit, Heft 4, 1935). Herder, Freiburg.

Koch, A.: Der neue Mythus und der alte Glaube. (Stimmen der Zeit, Heft 2, Nov. 1934). Herder, Freiburg.

Königer-Böckenhoff: Katholische Kirche und moderner Staat. Köln 1920.

Kother, F.: Vom Geheimnis der Papstkirche. J. Bercker, Kevelaer 1934.

Kraemer, H.: Das 19. Jahrhundert in Wort und Bild. Bong, Berlin-Leipzig.

Kralik, R.: Allgem. Geschichte der Neuesten Zeit.

Krauss, F.: Cavour. Mainz 1902.

Krüger, G.: Das Papsttum. Seine Idee und ihre Träger. J. C. B. Mohr, Tübingen 1932.

Kuypers, F.: Spanien unter Kreuz und Halbmond. Klinkhardt & Biermann, Leipzig 1917.

Labanca, B.: Die Zukunft des Papsttums. (Deutsch v. Sell, M.). Tübingen 1906.

Landsberg: Die Welt des Mittelalters und Wir. Bonn 1923.

Lange, C. und Dreyer, E.: Deutscher Geist 1935. Kulturdokumente der Gegenwart. R. Voigtländer, Leipzig 1934.

Langen, J.: Geschichte der römischen Kirche. Bonn 1881-93.

Langer, W.: The Franco-Russian Alliance 1890-1894. Harvard University Press, Cambridge 1929.

Lasson, G.: Zur Theorie des christlichen Dogmas. Berlin 1897.

Lecanuet, E.: Les premières annés du pontificat de Léon XIII. (1878-94). Paris 1931.

Lecanuet, E.: La vie de l'Eglise de France sous Léon XIII. Paris 1930.

Lefebvre de Béheine: Léon XIII. et le prince de Bismarck. Paris 1898.

Leiber, R.: Geschichte der Päpste im 19. Jahrhundert. Herder, Freiburg 1933.

Lennhoff, E.: Die Freimaurer. Amalthea-Verlag, Wien 1929.

Leo XIII.: Carmina (herausg v. G. Brunelli). Udine 1883.

Leo XIII.: Acta Leonis XIII. Rome 1881/1903.

Leo-Gesellschaft: Die katholische Kirche unserer Zeit und ihre Diener in Wort und Bild. Wien 1899.

Löffler, K.: Papstgeschichte von der Französischen Revolution bis zur Gegenwart. Kösel, München-Kempten 1911.

Lucka, E.: Urgut der Menschheit.

Lucka, E.: Die Verwandlung des Menschen. Rascher, Zürich 1934.

Lugmayer, K.: Leos XIII. Lösung der Arbeiterfrage. 1927.

Lugmayer, K.: Die gesellschaftlichen Rundschreiben Leos XIII. und seiner unmittelbaren Vorgänger. Wien 1930.

Lulvès, J.: Bismarck und die Römische Frage. (Hochland, Heft 9/1928/1929). Kösel, München-Kempten.

Lutz, H.: Christentum und Deutschreligion. Bonifacius-Druckerei, Paderborn 1934.

Maistre, J. de: Du Pape. 1854.

Marcks, S., und Müller, K.: Meister der Politik. Eine weltgeschichtliche Reihe von Bildnissen. Deutsche Verlags-Anst., Stuttgart 1923.

Martens, P.: Geheime Gesellschaften in alter und neuer Zeit. F. E. Baumann, Leipzig.

Mausbach: Die Religion und das moderne Seelenleben. München 1923.

Mauthner, F.: Der Atheismus und seine Geschichte im Abendlande. Deutsche Verlags-Anst., Stuttgart 1922.

Mensi-Klarbach, A.: Vor und hinter den Kulissen der Welt- und Kulturgeschichte. Parcus, München 1925.

Mereschkowskij, D.: Napoleon. Th. Knaur, Berlin 1928.

Meyer, H.: Geschichte der alten Philosophie. Kösel & Pustet, München 1925.

Meyer, Th.: Die christlich-ethischen Sozialprinzipien und die Arbeiterfrage. Herder, Freiburg 1904.

Michel, E.: Kirche und Wirklichkeit. Ein katholisches Zeitbuch. E. Diederichs, Jena 1923.

Miller, O.: Der Individualismus als Schicksal. Herder, Freiburg 1933.

Monts, A.: Erinnerungen und Gedanken des Botschafters Anton Graf Monts. Verl. f. Kulturpolitik, Berlin 1932.

Muckermann, F.: Vom Rätsel der Zeit. Kösel & Pustet, München 1933.

Müller, A.: Papst und Kurie. Halle 1922.

Müller-Freienfels, R.: Metaphysik des Irrationalem. F. Meiner, Leipzig 1927.

Müller-Freienfels, R.: Irrationalismus. Umrisse einer Erkenntnislehre. F. Meiner, Leipzig.

Müller-Freienfels, R.: Die Philosophie des 20. Jahrhunderts. Mittler & Sohn, Berlin.

Münz, S.: Römische Reminiscenzen und Profile. Allgemeiner Verein für Deutsche Literatur. Berlin 1900.

Mutius, G. v.: Zur Mythologie der Gegenwart. E. Reinhardt, München 1933.

Narfon, J.: Léon XIII. intime. Paris.

[193]

Nielson, F.: Geschichte des Papsttums im 19. Jahrhundert. Gotha 1880.

Nowak, C.: Geschichte des zweiten Kaiserreiches. Verlag f. Kulturpolitik, Berlin.

Nürnberger: Zur Kirchengeschichte des 19. Jahrhunderts. Mainz 1897 bis 1900.

O'Reilly Bachem: Leo XIII. Seine Zeit, sein Pontifikat und seine Erfolge. Köln 1887.

Orsi, P.: Das moderne Italien. Geschichte der lezten 150 Jahre bis zum Ende des 19. Jahrh. B. G. Teubner, Leipzig 1902.

Pachtler, S.: Der stille Krieg gegen Thron und Altar. Habbell, Amberg 1873.

Pachtler, S.: Der Götze der Humanität. Herder, Freiburg 1875.

Das Papsttum in Bildern: Kösel & Pustet, München.

Die Papstwahl, eine Beschreibung und Abbildung der Gebräuche usw. Augsburg 1846.

Pastor, L.: History of the Popes from the Close of the Middle Ages. B. Herder & Co., St. Louis 1912.

Pflugk-Harttung, H.: Weltgeschichte. (Sammelwerk). Ullstein, Berlin 1909.

Propyläen-Weltgeschichte. Propyläen-Verlag, Berlin.

Przywara, E.: Katholizismus der Kirche und Katholizismus der Stunde. (Stimmen der Zeit, 4. Heft, Jänner 1926). Herder, Freiburg.

Ranke, L.: Die römischen Päpste in den letzten vier Jahrhunderten. Phaidon-Verlag, Wien 1933.

Reik, Th.: Dogma und Zwangsidee. Int. Psychoanalyt. Verlag, Wien 1927.

Reinarz, H.: Von Ketteler und Leo XIII. Der soziale Bischof und der soziale Papst des 19. Jahrh. L. Schwann, Düsseldorf 1931.

Reinhold, G.: Der alte und der neue Glaube. H. Kirsch, Wien 1909.

Reisner, E.: Das Selbstopfer der Erkenntnis. Eine Betrachtung über die Kulturaufgabe der Philosophie.

Reisner, E.: Die Geschichte als Sündenfall und Weg zum Gericht. Grundlage einer christlichen Metaphysik d. Geschichte.

Renan, E.: Averroes et l'Averroisme. A. Durand, Paris 1852.

Reumont, A.: Geschichte der Stadt Rom. Berlin 1867-70.

Roepke, F.: Von Gambetta bis Clemenceau. Deutsche Verlags-Anstalt, Stuttgart 1922.

Rohden, P. und Ostrogorsky, G.: Menschen, die Geschichte machten. L. W. Seidel, Wien 1931.

Rolfes, E.: Die Philosophie des Thomas von Aquin. F. Meiner, Leipzig 1920.

Rolfes, E.: Die Philosophie des Aristoteles. F. Meiner, Leipzig 1923.

Rössle, W.: Heroische Politik. Jena 1934.

Rössler, O.: Grundriss einer Geschichte Roms im Mittelalter. Berlin 1909.

Rüschkampf, F.: Das Vatikanische Konzil — heute. (Stimmen der Zeit, 5. Heft, Febr. 1934). Herder, Freiburg.

Sabatier, A.: Die Religion und die moderne Kultur. (Vortrag auf dem ersten religionswissenschaftlichen Kongress zu Stockholm). J. C. B. Mohr, Tübingen 1898.

Schaepmann, H.: Leo XIII. Ein Charakter-und Zeitbild. Theissingsche Buchhdlg., Münster 1893.

Schell: Der Katholizismus als Prinzip des Fortschritts. Würzburg 1899.

Schilling, O.: Die Staats- u. Soziallehre des Papstes Leo XIII. 1925.

Schlichter: Unseres Heiligen Vaters Papst Leo XIII. Leben, Münster.

Schlözer, K. v.: Letzte römische Briefe (1882-94). Deutsche Verlags-Anstalt, Stuttgart 1924.

Schmidlin, J.: Papstgeschichte der neuesten Zeit. Kösel & Pustet, München 1934.

Schmidlin, J.: Papsttum und Päpste gegenüber den modernen Strömungen. Kösel & Pustet, München 1934.

Schneemann: Der Papst, das Oberhaupt der Gesamtkirche. Freiburg 1867.

Schneider, F.: Rom und Romgedanke. 1926.

Schneider, M.: Leo XIII., sein Leben und Wirken. Kempten 1903.

Schnürer, G.: Kirche und Kultur im Mittelalter. F. Schöningh, Paderborn 1926.

Schreiner, H.: Ehre und Glaube. Wicher-Verlag, Berlin 1934.

Schwemer, R.: Papsttum und Kaisertum. Stuttgart 1899.

Schwer, W.: Papst Leo XIII. Herder, Freiburg 1923.

Schwerdt, F.: Papst Leo XIII. Ein Blick auf seine Jugend und seine Dichtungen. Augsburg 1887.

Seeberg, R.: Lehrbuch der Dogmengeschichte. A. Deichert, Leipzig. Erlangen 1920.

Seignobos, Ch.: A Political History of Europe since 1814. Henry Holt & Co., New York 1895.

Seppelt, F., und Löffler, K.: Papstgeschichte von den Anfängen bis zur Gegenwart. Kösel & Pustet, München 1933.

Seppelt, F., und Löffler, K.: Der Aufstieg des Papsttums. Geschichte der Päpste von den Anfängen bis zum Regierungsantritt Gregors des Grossen. J. Hegner, Leipzig, 1931.

Serclaes, O.: Le pape Léon XIII. 1907.

Sinopoli di Giunta, G.: Kardinal Mariano Rampolla del Tindaro. F. Borgmeyer, Hildesheim 1929.

Smolka, St. v.: Erinnerung an Leo XIII. Herder, Freiburg 1906.

Soderini, E.: The Pontificate of Leo XIII. Burns, Oates & Washbourne. London 1934.

Soderini, E.: Leo XIII. und der deutsche Kulturkampf. Tyrolia, Wien.

Sombart, W.: Der Bourgeois. Dunker & Humblot, München-Leipzig 1913.

Sorel, G.: Uber die Gewalt. Wagner, Innsbruck 1928.

Spahn, M.: Leo XIII. Kirchheim, München 1905.

Spahn, M.: Der Untergang des Kirchenstaats und Leo XIII. (Hochland, Heft 1, 1912/13). Kösel, München-Kempten.

Steinbüchel: Der Zweckgedanke bei Thomas von Aquin.

Strich, W.: Der irrationale Mensch. L. Schneider, Berlin 1928.

Stutz, O.: Die päpstliche Diplomatie unter Leo XIII. Erinnerungen des Kardinals Ferrata. 1926.

Tessenberg-Wesierski, F.: Wesen und Bedeutung des Zweifelns. Breslau 1928.

Thomas Aquinas: Summa Theologica. English edition, edited by English Dominicans. Burns, Oates and Washbourne, London.

Tillich, P.: Protestantismus als Kritik und Gestaltung. O. Reichl, Darmstadt 1929.

Tischleder, P.: Die Staatslehre Leos XIII. 1925.

Traub, G.: Materialien zum Verständnis und zur Kritik des katholischen Sozialismus. München 1902.

Troeltsch: Die Soziallehren der christlichen Kirchen. Tübingen 1919.

Ulitzka, K.: Leo XIII., der Lehrer der Welt, neue praktische Ausgabe der wichtigsten Enzykliken Leos XIII. Bernau in der Mark 1903.

Varga, L.: Das Schlagwort vom "Finsteren Mittelalter." R. N. Rohrer, Baden-Wien-Leipzig 1932.

Vigener: Ketteler. Ein deutsches Bischofsleben des 19. Jahrh. München-Berlin 1923.

Waal, A. de: Unseres Heiligen Vaters Papst Leos XIII. Leben. A. Russel, Münster.

Waentig, H., u. Gehrig, H.: Belgiens Volkswirtschaft. B. G. Teubner, Leipzig-Berlin 1918.

Wattenbach, W.: Geschichte des römischen Papsttums. Berlin 1876.

Wehberg, H.: Das Papsttum und der Weltfriede. M. Gladbach 1915.

Wells, H. G.: Outline of History. Doubleday, New York 1931.

White, A. D.: History of the Warfare of Science with Theology in Christendom. Appleton, New York.

Wiegler, P.: Wilhelm der Erste. Sein Leben und seine Zeit. Avalun-Verlag, Hellerau 1927.

Wilhelm II: Ereignisse und Gestalten aus den Jahren 1878-1918. K. F. Koehler. Leipzig-Berlin 1922.

Zach, F.: Modernes oder katholisches Kulturideal? Herder, Freiburg 1925.

Zacher, A.: Aus Vatikan und Quirinal. Bilder vom Nebeneinanderleben der beiden Höfe. Frankfurt a. M. 1901.

Ziegler, Th.: Die geistigen und sozialen Strömungen des 19. Jahrhunderts. G. Bondi, Berlin 1899.

INDEX

Æterni Patris, encyclical, 61, 70-3, 81, 166-7.
Alexander of Hales, 11.
Alfonso VI, King of Spain, 10.
Anaxagoras, Greek philosopher, 142.
Anselm of Canterbury, 68, 145.
Anti-council of Free-Thinkers, Naples (1869), 6-8, 18, 24-5, 26.
Antonelli, Cardinal, papal secretary of State, 56.
Arabian interpreters of Aristotle, 9, 10, 11, 62, 63.
Arian heresy, 21.
Aristotle: mediæval revival of philosophy, 9-11, 62; mediæval opposition to, 18-19; revolt against in 17th century, 141-5, 169; revival of scholasticism under Pope Leo XIII, 61 *et seq;* modern objections to philosophy not new, 172-6, 181.
Armada, Spanish, 91.
Athens, Academy of, 177, 179.
Augusta, Empress of Germany, 95.
Augustine, Saint, 66, 76, 77.
Augustinian canons, opposition to scholasticism, 10-11.
Austria, 92, 95.
Averroes (Ibn-Roshd), 11, 63, 64, 69.

Bacon, Francis, Baron Verulam, 142, 143, 144, 174, 175, 179.
Bayle, Pierre, 18.
Bebel, August, 127.
Beghards, 21.
Belgium, 49, 54-6, 100.
Benedict XV, 155, 156, 157-8.
Benevento, 54.
Bertani, Masonic leader, 97.
Bismarck, Otto von, 35, 83, 86, 87-90, 93, 94, 108, 109.
Bolshevism, 159 *et seq.*
Boniface VIII, Pope, 85.

Bruges, 49.
Bruno, Giordano, 101, 142, 182.
Bulls: *In eminenti,* of Pope Clement XII, 19; *Unam sanctam* of Boniface VIII, 85.
Bülow, Prince Bernhard von, 59.

Canossa, 84.
Caroline Islands, 93.
Carpineto, 45, 53, 64.
Carthusian monks, expelled from France, 100.
Centre, German party, 89, 94.
Chalcedon, Council of, 23.
Chiwi, Jewish philosopher, 63-4.
Civitas Dei, 83.
Clémenceau, Georges, 148.
Clement XII, Pope, 19.
College of Cardinals, 37, 150.
Combes, Emile, French premier, 157.
Comte, Auguste, 26, 96, 97, 171, 176.
Conclave, papal, 37, 150.
"Constitution of the Catholic Faith," 3.
Constitution *Pastor æternus,* 4, 5.
Coucon, Robert de, 19.
Crispi, Francesco, 97-8, 112, 113, 182.
Critique of Reason, by Kant, 13.
Czechoslovakia, 157.

Darwinism, 173, 175.
Democritus, Greek philosopher, 142, 172-3, 175.
Descartes, René, 11, 63, 141, 173, 175, 179.
Devas, English sociologist, 137.
Diderot, Denis, 12.
Dietrichstein, Count, 55.
Döllinger, Ignaz von, 29.
Dostoevsky, Feodor Mikhailovich, 35, 36, 109.
Dreyfus affair, 148.

Driesch, Hans, 173-4.
Dumas, Alexander, 98.
Dupanloup, Félix Antoine Philibert, French bishop, 27, 28.
Duport, Adrien, French revolutionary, 181-2.

Economics: attitude of mediævalism to, 17-18, 75-6; rise of industrialism, 48-50; encyclical *Rerum novarum*, 121 et seq., 154-5; and World War, 155-6; encyclical *Quadragesimo anno*, 161 et seq.
Ecumenical Council, 21.
Education, conflict b e t w e e n Church and State on, 99-100.
Encyclicals of Pope Leo XIII: *Inscrutabili Deo Consilio*, 43, 81; *Æterni Patris*, 61, 70-3, 81, 166-7; *Libertas*, 73-5; *Pervenuti*, 81; *Humanum genus* (on Freemasonry), 101 et seq.; *Sapientiæ Christianæ*, 92-3, 110, 115; *Rerum novarum*, 121, 154-5, 161-2, 176; *Quod apostolici muneris*, 128; *Graves de commune*, 137-8.
of Pope Pius X: *Pascendi*, 153.
of Pope Pius XI: *Quadragesimo anno*, 161 et seq., 167.
Engels, Friedrich, 126.
England, relations with Papacy, 91-2, 95, 116.
"Enlightenment," 11, 12, 25, 145, 171-2.
Entelechy, scholastic doctrine of, 76, 147, 173-4.

Falk, Paul Ludwig Adalbert, Prussian Minister of Education, 88.
Fascism, 182 et seq.
Fauché-Borel, Louis, 97.
Feuerbach, Anselm, 124.
Finland, 157.
Fitzgerald, Edward, A m e r i c a n bishop, 28.
Flaubert, Gustave, 34, 35.
Fornari, Monseigneur, papal nuncio to Brussels, 55, 56.
France, relations with Vatican,
96, 97-8, 100, 109-11, 148-9, 152, 157.
France, Anatole, 148.
Francis Joseph, Austrian emperor, 150.
Frederick Barbarossa, 84.
Frederick II, of Germany (the Great), 35.
Freemasons, 18, 19, 25, 97, 101 et seq., 113, 119.
Free-Thinkers, 97. *See also* Anticouncil of Free-Thinkers.
French Revolution, 29-30.
Frohschammer, Jakob, 15.

Galileo (Galilei), 63, 143, 175.
Galimberti, Monseigneur, 95, 115.
Gambetta, Léon, 98, 108, 109, 111, 119.
Garibaldi, Joseph, 97.
Gasparri, Cardinal, papal secretary of State, 160.
Georg, Stefan, 60.
Germany: relations with Vatican, 88-90, 93-5, 99-100, 114, 116; fascism in, 183.
Giers, Russian foreign minister, 117.
Gladstone, William Ewart, 25, 90-2, 95.
Grande Chartreuse, 100.
Graves de commune, encyclical, 137-8.
Gregorian chant, restoration of, 154.
Gregory VII, Pope, 84.
Gregory IX, Pope, 19, 64, 168.
Gregory XVI, Pope, 19-20, 38-9, 54, 56, 64, 100.
Greith, bishop of St. Gall, 27.
Günther, Anton, 15.

Hapsburgs, 87.
Hegel, Georg, 121.
Henry IV, German Emperor, 84.
Henry VIII, King of England, 91.
Hermes, Georg, 15.
Holbach, Paul Heinrich Dietrich von, 13.
Holland, relations with Vatican, 156.

Moriarty, English bishop, 27.
Mueller-Frienfels, Richard, 174.
Mun, Count de, 136.
Murri, Romolo, 149, 153.
Music, reform of Church, 154.

Napoleon Bonaparte, 30-2, 47, 139.
National socialism, 183-4.
Nestorius, author of heresy, 21.
Newman, John Henry Cardinal, 27.
Nicaea, Council of, 21.
Nietzsche, Friedrich, 180, 181.
Nothomb, Belgian minister, 55-6.

O'Connell, Daniel, Irish liberator, 91.
"Old Catholics," of Germany, 29.

Papacy: infallibility of, 4 *et seq.*; 27-9, 92; Thomistic ideas regarding, 5; and modern thought, 39; fixity on principle, 43-4; and secular power, 83 *et seq.* See *also* Roman Question.
Papal States, 45, 51.
Parma, Grand Duke of, 2.
Pascendi, encyclical of Pope Pius X, 153.
Pecci, Colonel Ludovico, 45.
Pereire, Isaac, 121.
Perugia, 40-1, 51, 52, 57.
Pervenuti, apostolic letter of Leo XIII, 81.
Philip Augustus, King of France, 85.
Pilate, 177, 178.
Pius VI, Pope, 30.
Pius VII, Pope (Barnaba Chiaramonti), 30-3, 47.
Pius IX, Pope: and Vatican Council, 1, 21-2, 80, 82, 91, 168; syllabus of errors, 20, 24, 64; fall of Rome, 34-6, 51, 103; and future Pope Leo XIII, 56, 58; and *Kulturkampf*, 88-90, and Austria, 92; and Belgium, 100; death, 103-4; lack of political talent, 108-9; and Polish revolt against Russia, 116.
Pius X, Pope: pontificate, 150 *et*

seq.; decrees and encyclicals, 153-4; and Thomism, 154-5.
Pius XI, Pope: and communism, 161; encyclical *Quadragesimo anno*, 161 *et seq.*
Plato, 76, 77, 172, 175.
Poland, revolt against Russia, 116-17, 157.
Portugal, 85.
Protagoras, 173.
Proudhon, Pierre-Joseph, 128.

Quadragesimo anno, encyclical, 161 *et seq.*, 176.
Quod apostolici muneris, encyclical of Pope Leo XIII, 128.

Race question, 185.
Rampolla, Mariano Cardinal, 81, 108, 115, 150, 157.
Ranke, Leopold von, 32.
Rattazzi, Signora, 58.
Reformation, 13, 21.
Renaissance, 13.
Rerum novarum, encyclical, 121 *et seq.*, 154-5, 161-2, 176.
Reisach, Cardinal Count, archbishop of Munich, 15-16.
Ricardo, David, 135.
Ricciardi, Giuseppe, 7.
Robespierre, Maximilien de, 176.
Rokitansky, Karl von, 24.
"Roman Question," 103 *et seq.*, 111-20.
Royalists, French, 110-11.
Ruffo-Scilla, papal nuncio, 95.
Russia: relations with Vatican, 115-18; rise of Bolshevism in, 159 *et seq.*

Saadja ben Joseph, 63.
Saint-Simon, Claude Henri de, 26, 96, 121.
Sangnier, Marc, 149.
Sapientiæ Christianæ, encyclical, 92-3, 110, 115, 116.
Sarto, Joseph Melchior. See Pius X, Pope.
Savoy, House of, 106.
Schlözer, Herr von, Prussian minister to Vatican, 118.

Date Due